Countdown
Seven Trumpets for Today

by Carol Zarska, MA in Religion

World rights reserved. This book or any portion thereof may not be copied or reproduced in any form or manner whatever, except as provided by law, without the written permission of the publisher, except by a reviewer who may quote brief passages in a review.

The author assumes full responsibility for the accuracy of all facts and quotations as cited in this book. The opinions expressed in this book are the author's personal views and interpretations, and do not necessarily reflect those of the publisher.

This book is provided with the understanding that the publisher is not engaged in giving spiritual, legal, medical, or other professional advice. If authoritative advice is needed, the reader should seek the counsel of a competent professional.

Copyright © 2016 TEACH Services, Inc.
ISBN-13: 978-1-4796-0579-8 (Paperback)
ISBN-13: 978-1-4796-0580-4 (ePub)
ISBN-13: 978-1-4796-0581-1 (Mobi)
Library of Congress Control Number: 2016900753

All scripture quotations, unless otherwise indicated, are taken from the New King James Version®. Copyright © 1982 by Thomas Nelson. Used by permission. All rights reserved.

Scripture quotations marked KJV are taken from the King James Version.

Published by

TEACH Services, Inc.
PUBLISHING
www.TEACHServices.com • (800) 367-1844

Prologue

There have always been times of special significance in human history. Kingdoms rise and fall, rulers come and go, wars rage, and nature is capricious in devastating storms and eruptions of earth and sea. Historically, the common man is scarcely aware of the great sweep of time beyond the daily routine of his life, and the inevitability that he will someday join the ranks of his ancestors who have passed on before him.

Today is not such a time. In the twenty-first century, events of such magnitude and frequency have occurred that there are few people around the globe who have not heard of these events and wondered what they mean. Interestingly, many are concluding that the end of all things is near. Fortunately, there are clues in the last book of the Bible that can give us direction and answers to the questions people are asking. There is a meaning to the apparently haphazard catastrophes that have been plaguing our planet. There is a divine plan, which is revealed in the book of Revelation. Through these prophecies we can discover where these events are leading us.

For centuries, the book of Revelation has been considered to be filled with symbols so difficult to decipher that it is impossible for us to comprehend the meaning, but the name itself indicates that it was written to be understood. It was written to guide humankind from the time Jesus ascended back to heaven and began His work in the heavenly sanctuary until He comes again in the clouds of glory. He instructed His disciples in Matthew 24 that although He was leaving them then, He would return at the end of the ages to take His waiting faithful followers back to be with Him forever. Since then, His people have looked with longing eyes for the signs of His coming. Centuries have come and gone, and now the signs are appearing in rapid succession.

It is the purpose of this book to alert the people of earth that time is running out. Jesus is soon to appear in the eastern sky! We can be among those who are awake and ready for His coming! But we must heed His counsel found in Luke 21:34-36:

> Be careful, or your hearts will be weighed down with carousing, drunkenness and the anxieties of life, and that day will close on you suddenly like a trap. For it will come on all those who live on the face of the whole earth. Be always on the watch, and pray that you may be able to escape all that is about to happen, and that you may be able to stand before the Son of Man.

May the things revealed in this book help each of us to be awake and prepared when He appears.

Contents

1: The Countdown Begins 7
2: Judgments on Land and Sea.. 16
3: The Descent Begins 25
4: Trumpets Then and Now.. 30
5: The Final Generation 39
6: God's Majestic Voice 45
7: Who Has the Mark? 53
8: Hands Across the Gulf... 59
9: Knowing the Time.. 67
10: The Appointed Time.. 76
11: The Hiding Place 84
12: Armageddon 96
Appendix: Miscellaneous Phenomena and Signs of the End 109
Bibliography 118

1 The Countdown Begins

Morning dawned bright and clear on that balmy September day in 2001. Not a cloud dotted the sky—nothing that would give the slightest warning that something was about to happen that would change the world forever. My phone rang. It was Sallie, a good friend and member of our church. "Have you heard what's happening?" she said.

"No," I answered. "Why?"

"Well, you had better get over to Christa's house and ask her to turn on her TV. Go *now*!" I didn't stop to question. The urgency in her voice seemed strangely ominous. What could be that important? I called Christa, instructed her to turn on the TV, hung up the phone, and headed for the door.

The three-minute walk through the trees to Christa's house seemed strangely calm. I felt as though I was surrounded by angels. A sacred hush was in the air. As I walked through the door into Christa's living room, I stood transfixed before the screen. Slowly I sat down and watched a scene that will forever be imbedded in my memory. The towers—the beautiful towers—airplanes crashing into them, smoke and fire billowing from the gashes made by the impact, and then the towers melting down as though they were made of plastic.

I don't remember any conversation with Christa; I only remember snatches of things that were said by speakers on the news broadcast. President Bush made a historic pronouncement that has been more than fulfilled. "We are at war," he said. "Nothing will ever be the same again." The news announcer called the war into which we were entering a "holy war" between the three great religions of the world—Christianity, Judaism, and Islam.

After two hours of watching the repeated scenes, I didn't feel a need to see anymore. As I was walking back home, I wondered if the scenes I had just seen were the same ones shown to Ellen G. White about the New York towers coming down. I walked directly to my bookcase and pulled out volume 9 of the *Testimonies for the Church*, and opened up the first chapter in the book, in which that vision was recorded. Strangely, the chapter begins on page 11. 9-11! I began to read:

> We are living in the time of the end. The fast-fulfilling signs of the times declare that the coming of Christ is near at hand. The days in which we live are solemn and important. The Spirit of God is gradually but surely being withdrawn from the earth. Plagues and judgments are already falling upon the despisers of the grace of God. The calamities by land and sea, the unsettled state of society, the alarms of war, are portentous. They forecast approaching events of the greatest magnitude. Great changes are soon to take place in our world, and the final movements will be rapid ones. The condition of things in the world shows that troublous times are right upon us....
>
> On one occasion, when in New York City, I was in the night season called upon to behold buildings rising story after story toward heaven. These buildings were warranted to be fire-proof, and they were erected to glorify their owners and builders. Higher and still higher these buildings rose, and in them the most costly material was used. Those to whom these buildings belonged were not asking themselves: "How can we best glorify God?" The Lord was not in their thoughts....
>
> The scene that next passed before me was an alarm of fire. Men looked at the lofty and supposedly fire-proof buildings and said: 'They are perfectly safe.' But these buildings were consumed as if made of pitch. The fire engines could do nothing to stay the destruction. The firemen were unable to operate the engines. I am instructed that when the Lord's time comes, should no change have taken place in the hearts of proud, ambitions human beings, men will find that the hand that had been strong to save will be strong to destroy. No earthly power can stay the hand of God. No material can be used in the erection of buildings that will preserve them from destruction when God's appointed time comes to send retribution on men for their disregard of His law and for their selfish ambition....
>
> But who reads the warnings given by the fast fulfilling signs of the times? What impression is made upon worldlings? What change is seen in their attitude? No more than was seen in the

attitude of the inhabitants of the Noachian world. Absorbed in worldly business and pleasure, the antediluvians 'knew not until the Flood came, and took them all away.' Matthew 24:39. They had heaven-sent warnings, but they refused to listen. And today the world, utterly regardless of the warning voice of God, is hurrying on to eternal ruin. The world is stirred with the spirit of war. The prophecy of the eleventh chapter of Daniel has nearly reached its complete fulfillment. Soon the scenes of trouble spoken of in the prophecies will take place....

'I am pained at my very heart; ... I cannot hold my peace, because thou has heard, O my soul, *the sound of the trumpet, the alarm of war*. Destruction upon destruction is cried; for the whole land is spoiled.' Jeremiah 4:19, 20. (*Testimonies for the Church*, vol. 9, pp. 11–15, emphasis added)

As I read the phrase, "the sound of the trumpet, the alarm of war," my mind went back to years before in my early experience of speaking for the Lord. For the first three and a half years of my career, I preached and taught only the topic of the Old Testament sanctuary as a model for prayer. Then the Lord began to impress upon my mind the importance of studying end-time events, especially the prophecies of Daniel and Revelation. I began to see evidences, especially through quotations from Ellen G. White, that prophecies from the past would be repeated and have special emphasis and meaning for the final generation. For example:

Each of the ancient prophets spoke less for their own time than for ours, so that their prophesying is in force for us.... The Bible has accumulated and bound up its treasures for the last generation. All the great events and solemn transactions of Old Testament history have been, and are, repeating themselves in the church in these last days. (*Selected Messages*, vol. 3, pp. 338, 339)

In the great final conflict, Satan will employ the same policy, manifest the same spirit, and work for the same end, as in all preceding ages. That which has been, will be, except that the coming struggle will be marked with a terrible intensity such as the world has never witnessed. (*The Great Controversy*, p. XI)

We are standing on the threshold of great and solemn events. Many of the prophecies are about to be fulfilled in quick succession. Every element of power is about to be set to work. Past history will be repeated; old controversies will arouse to new life, and peril will beset God's people on every side. Intensity is taking hold of the human family. It is permeating everything upon the earth.... Study Revelation in connection with Daniel, for history will be repeated. (*Testimonies to Ministers and Gospel Workers*, p. 116)

As I studied the prophecies of Revelation, I could see how the experience of the seven churches, which are recorded in chapters two and three, could have significance and counsel for the church at the end of time. All the problems that have already taken place seem to be present once again in some form or another in the church today. In addition, the prophetic view of the seven seals of Revelation six could also apply to God's remnant church, who, coming fresh from the reception of the latter rain, will go forth in the power of God to preach the loud cry, just as the early church preached the gospel under the power of the early rain.

However, as I read the description of the seven trumpets of chapters eight and nine, I could see no possible application to the end of time. Growing up as a Seventh-day Adventist, and going to our schools from second grade through college, I was very aware of the historic view of the trumpets. This view covers the ancient time period that begins with the four stages of the fall of Rome and ends with the opening of the investigative judgment in 1844. Yet I could see no possible implications that would apply to the final generation. As I prayed about this question and asked God for enlightenment, the impression that I would know it when it happened came to my mind.

Years went by, and I thought no more about the trumpets, until that balmy, fall day in September 2001—the day that changed the world forever and began the countdown toward eternity. Walk with me, if you will, through the journey that we have all taken since that day, and see in the light of prophecy how God is warning the world of the nearness of His coming. What a wonderful, loving God He is to let us hear His footsteps as He prepares everyone who will listen to be ready to meet Him in peace!

Let's go back now to the text in Jeremiah 4:19, which Ellen G. White quoted in connection with the troublous times of the end, including the falling of the towers in New York City. The important phrase is, "the sound of the trumpet, the alarm of war." This is a direct reference to the use of trumpets in the Old Testament, found in Numbers 10:1–9:

The LORD said to Moses: 'Make two trumpets of hammered silver, and use them for calling the community together and for having the camps set out. When both are sounded, the whole community is to assemble before you at the entrance to the tent of meeting. If only one is sounded, the leaders—the heads of the clans of Israel—are to assemble before you.... The blast will be the signal for setting out. To gather the assembly, blow the trumpets, but not with the same signal for setting out. The sons of Aaron, the priests, are to blow the trumpets. This is to be a lasting ordinance for you and the generations to come. When you go into battle in your own land against an enemy who is oppressing you, sound a blast on the trumpets. Then you will be remembered by the LORD your God and rescued from your enemies.'

Ellen G. White also has some very important comments about the meaning and the importance of the trumpets. For instance, she says in *Patriarchs and Prophets*, "The sound of a trumpet summoned Israel to meet with God" (p. 339). She continues in the first volume of *Testimonies for the Church*:

The Levites were designated by the Lord as the tribe in the midst of whom the sacred ark was to be borne, Moses and Aaron marching just in front of the ark, and the sons of Aaron following near them, each bearing trumpets. They were to receive directions from Moses, which they were to signify to the people by speaking through the trumpets. These trumpets gave special sounds which the people understood, and directed their movements accordingly.... None who gave attention were left in ignorance of what they were to do. If any failed to comply with the requirements of the Lord ... they were punished with death.... For they would only prove themselves willingly ignorant.... If they did not know the will of God concerning them, it was their own fault. They had the same opportunities to obtain the knowledge imparted as others ... had, therefore their sin of not knowing, not understanding, was as great in the sight of God as if they had heard and then transgressed. (p. 651)

It would seem, then, that the subject of the trumpets is of vital importance for God's people, even today. We should do everything possible to learn the present-day meaning of God's warning messages for our time. A contemporary Seventh-day Adventist author, C. Mervyn Maxwell, puts it this way in the second volume of his book, *God Cares*, "The seven trumpets of Revelation represent scourges, wars, and judgments." (p. 236). He says that they are to be seen as " 'warning judgments.' People who learn the lessons the trumpets are designed to teach won't have to suffer the catastrophic judgments of the seven last plagues. ... They constitute *severe* judgment warnings.... Their purpose [is] to persuade the 'rest of mankind' to 'repent'" (p. 224). He also notes, "Ancient prophets taught that disasters, like trumpets, call for repentance" (p. 234).

What are these warnings trying to tell us? Inasmuch as the trumpets seem to be a succession of warnings, each increasing in severity until the seventh trumpet announces the setting up of God's eternal kingdom (Rev. 11:15; 1 Cor. 15:51, 52; Matt. 24:30–34), I would like to suggest that the trumpets represent the gradual withdrawal of God's protection from an impenitent world. It is a clear expression of His efforts to arouse those who will take His warnings to heart and flee to the safety of His pavilion.

"The Spirit of the Lord is being withdrawn from the earth. Were it not that God has commanded angelic agencies to control the satanic agencies that are seeking to break loose and to destroy, there would be no hope. But the winds are to be held until the servants of God are sealed in their foreheads" (*In Heavenly Places*, p. 96).

The gradual withdrawal of God's special favor and protection has a precedent in the writings of Ezekiel:

> I looked, and I saw the likeness of a throne of lapis lazuli above the vault that was over the heads of the cherubim. The LORD said to the man clothed in linen, "Go in among the wheels beneath the cherubim. Fill your hands with burning coals from among the cherubim and scatter them over the city." And as I watched, he went in. (Ezek. 10:1, 2)

Volume four of *The Seventh-day Adventist Bible Commentary*, p. 609 states that the act of scattering the burning coals symbolizes "the impending destruction of the city'. Perhaps a similar meaning, encompassing the whole world, could apply to the throne room scene in Revelation 8:2–6, which announces the blowing of the seven trumpets:

> And I saw the seven angels who stand before God, and seven trumpets were given to them. Another angel, who had a golden censer, came and stood at the altar. He was given much incense to offer, with the prayers of God's people, on the golden altar in front of the throne.... Then the angel took the censer, filled

it with fire from the altar, and hurled it on the earth; and there came peals of thunder, rumblings, flashes of lightning and an earthquake. Then the seven angels who had the seven trumpets prepared to sound them.

It is interesting to note that the trumpets begin to blow when the censer filled with the prayers of the saints is thrown down upon the earth. God's people for centuries have been praying and longing for the final end of the reign of sin. Like the martyrs in Revelation 6:10, they cry out, "How long, Sovereign Lord, holy and true, until you judge the inhabitants of the earth and avenge our blood?" But they must wait for that final generation who will fully cooperate with Jesus, as He cleanses His people through His closing ministry in the heavenly sanctuary.

Going back to the withdrawal of God's Spirit from the earthly sanctuary, Ezekiel chronicles the four stages:

> Now the cherubim were standing on the south side of the temple when the man went in, and a cloud filled the inner court. Then the glory of the LORD rose from above the cherubim and moved to the threshold of the temple. The cloud filled the temple, and the court was full of the radiance of the glory of the LORD.... Then the glory of the LORD departed from over the threshold of the temple and stopped above the cherubim. While I watched, the cherubim spread their wings and rose from the ground, and as they went, the wheels went with them. They stopped at the entrance to the east gate of the LORD's house, and the glory of the God of Israel was above them. (Ezek. 10:3, 4; 18, 19)

He continues:

> Then the cherubim, with the wheels beside them, spread their wings, and the glory of the God of Israel was above them. The glory of the LORD went up from within the city and stopped above the mountain east of it.... Then the vision I had seen went up from me, and I told the exiles everything the LORD had shown me. (Ezek. 11:22–25)

This final stage of the withdrawal of God's Spirit can be a great comfort to us in the days ahead. God's true people have always hidden in the rocks and mountains for safety from their enemies. When the followers of Jesus fled from Jerusalem prior to its destruction in AD 70, they found refuge in the mountains, as Jesus had instructed them in Matthew 24:16. So it will be for God's remnant just before Jesus comes again. His Spirit will abide with them and His angels will protect them through the time of trouble. They will be hidden under the shadow of His wings (see Ps. 91).

Please notice that there are four stages of the withdrawal of the Holy Spirit from the sanctuary. This division of four has an important significance for the meaning of the trumpets, which we will consider more thoroughly later. The most important concept to understand now is that time is running out for the people of earth! The seventh trumpet is the second coming of Jesus! The question to consider is this: where are we on the countdown toward the most significant event in the history of humankind?

> Satan is now using every device in this sealing time to keep the minds of God's people from the present truth and to cause them to waver. I saw a covering that God was drawing over His people to protect them in the time of trouble; and every soul that was decided on the truth and was pure in heart was to be covered with the covering of the Almighty.... I saw that many were neglecting the preparation so needful and were looking to the time of 'refreshing' and the 'latter rain' to fit them to stand in the day of the Lord and to live in His sight. Oh, how many I saw in the time of trouble without a shelter! They had neglected the needful preparation; therefore they could not receive the refreshing that all must have to fit them to live in the sight of a holy God. (*Early Writings*, pp. 43, 71)

Brothers and sisters, I believe that our long-suffering and merciful God, who does not want even one soul to be lost, is now using the events that are transpiring upon the earth to awaken all who will listen and take heed. Unfortunately, so few know what they portend or how little preparation time is left. We have almost become numb to tragedy and immune to the meaning of the momentous times in which we live.

Only God can see when the harvest of the earth is ripe and when it is time to put in the sickle and reap. But when that moment arrives, nothing can stop Him from bringing the great controversy to a close. But we can—and must—recognize when the time is near. This is the purpose for the seven trumpets for our time.

> Then another angel came out of the temple and called in a loud voice to him who was sitting on the cloud, 'Take your sickle and reap, because the time to reap has come, for the harvest of the

earth is ripe.' So he who was seated on the cloud swung his sickle over the earth, and the earth was harvested. Another angel came out of the temple in heaven, and he too had a sharp sickle. Still another angel, who had charge of the fire, came from the altar and called in a loud voice to him who had the sharp sickle, 'Take your sharp sickle and gather the clusters of grapes from the earth's vine, because its grapes are ripe.' The angel swung his sickle on the earth, gathered its grapes and threw them into the great winepress of God's wrath. (Rev. 14:15–19)

Here we see two distinct stages of the harvest. Jesus first reaps His own people and places them forever safe within the protection of the heavenly angels. Then an angel is delegated to bring about the seven last plagues, as recorded in Revelation chapters 15 and 16. Thus, during the warning time of the trumpets, God separates out His own people who hear and understand the meaning of the events that are transpiring. But most of the inhabitants of earth will be found unready when the curtain of probationary time comes down and the extension of God's mercy has ended.

"God permits the wicked to prosper and to reveal their enmity against Him, that when they shall have filled up the measure of their iniquity all may see His justice and mercy in their utter destruction" (*The Great Controversy*, p. 48). Understanding the trumpets, then, is vital to God's people at this time. The hour is already late. Wake up, sleeping virgins, for the wedding of the Bridegroom and His bride is about to begin!

2 Judgments on Land and Sea

When I first began to study the trumpets after the fall of the New York towers, I assumed that God would reveal to me each trumpet in succession as they happened, but that was not to be the case. As I read the Bible, I began to see correlations in Old Testament Scriptures through which God opened my mind to understand the outline and meaning of the other trumpets. Oh, how precious is the privilege of reading the Word of God and perceiving the truths that He has in store for each one of us to bless us personally!

> The Holy Spirit is beside every true searcher of God's Word, enabling him to discover the hidden gems of truth. Divine illumination comes to his mind, stamping the truth upon him with a new, fresh importance. He is filled with a joy never before felt. The peace of God rests upon him. The preciousness of truth is realized as never before. A heavenly light shines upon the Word, making it appear as though every letter were tinged with gold. God Himself speaks to the heart, making His Word spirit and life. (*Reflecting Christ*, p. 128)

> The words of God are the wellsprings of life. As you seek unto those living springs you will, through the Holy Spirit, be brought into communion with Christ. Familiar truths will present themselves to your mind in a new aspect, texts of Scripture will burst upon you with a new meaning as a flash of light, you will see the relation of other truths to the work of redemption, and you will know that Christ is leading you, a divine Teacher is at your side. (*Thoughts from the Mount of Blessing*, p. 20)

So within a few months, I wrote an article on everything that God had revealed to me, and I began to share it with a few other people. Because it was placed in the future, it did not arouse much interest. So I waited for the events to transpire, sharing only with a few close friends and loved ones. Here is a simple outline of how I understood the trumpets in those early months after the fall of the towers:

> #1. The Fall of the Towers
> #2. Natural Disasters
> #3. The Fall of America
> #4. Sunday Law Movement
> #5. War with Islam
> #6. War Escalating; Close of Probation; Armageddon
> #7. Jesus' Coming

Using this outline, I will now record the Scripture texts and/or Spirit of Prophecy quotations and other sources that had meaning to me as I studied each trumpet in its order. I am including only the parts of the texts that were the most significant to me.

#1. The Fall of the Towers

> *The first angel sounded his trumpet*, and there came hail and fire mixed with blood, and it was hurled down on the earth. (Rev. 8:7, emphasis added)

> Hail, fire, and blood taken together characterize warfare. (*God Cares*, Vol 2, p. 237)

> Announce in Judah and proclaim in Jerusalem and say: 'Sound the trumpet throughout the land!' Cry aloud and say: 'Gather together! Let us flee to the fortified cities!' Raise the signal to go to Zion! Flee for safety without delay! For I am bringing disaster from the north, even terrible destruction. A lion has come out of his lair; a destroyer of nations has set out. He has left his place to lay waste your land.... 'A scorching wind from the barren heights in the desert blows toward my people, but not to winnow or cleanse; a wind too strong for that comes from me. Now I pronounce my judgments against them.' Look! He advances like the clouds, his chariots come like a whirlwind, his horses are swifter than eagles. Woe to us! We are ruined! Jerusalem,

wash the evil from your heart and be saved.... Oh, the agony of my heart! My heart pounds within me, I cannot keep silent. For I have heard the sound of the trumpet; I have heard the battle cry. (Jer. 4:5–19)

The last verse is the same one that was quoted by Ellen White in *Testimonies for the Church*, vol. 9, p. 15: "I am pained at my very heart.... I cannot hold my peace, because thou hast heard, O my soul, the sound of the trumpet, the alarm of war" (Jer. 4:19, KJV). It seemed significant to me that this was quoted by her in conjunction with end-time disasters, including the falling of the towers.

> In the day of great slaughter, when the towers fall, streams of water will flow on every high mountain and every lofty hill. (Isa. 30:25)

> In the last days, God says, I will pour out my Spirit on all people. Your sons and daughters will prophesy, your young men will see visions, your old men will dream dreams. Even on my servants, both men and women, I will pour out my Spirit in those days, and they will prophesy. I will show wonders in the heaven above and signs on the earth below, blood and fire and billows of smoke. The sun will be turned to darkness and the moon to blood before the coming of the great and glorious day of the Lord. And everyone who calls on the name of the Lord will be saved. (Acts 2:17–21)

My conclusion from the texts above was that the falling of the towers would be the beginning of a series of end-time events whose purpose would be to alert the world of the coming of Jesus.

#2. Natural Disasters

On Sunday, November 17, 2002, two years before the catastrophes of the second trumpet began, Karen, my daughter, shared with me a special experience that she had with Jesus while spending some time in prayer earlier that afternoon. She had been fasting that day, and her communion with God was especially close. As her heart reached out for a closer connection to Jesus, she felt Him say,

> *I am coming personally to direct the events of the second trumpet, bringing with Me a retinue of the highest angels in heaven to assist*

Me in the work which I must do. It will be like other times when Earth's wickedness reached a crisis point, and I had to intervene to protect My people and My eternal plan. At those times I came personally to direct the battle against evil—such times as before the flood, at the tower of Babel, and at the destruction of Sodom and Gomorrah. This is one of those crisis times when I must personally intervene. Even now I am on My way. This is why many of you have been feeling that something is about to happen. This is why I have been asking you to fast and pray more than usual and to walk carefully before Me, not deviating from My will and My presence in even the smallest details of your life. I must have witnesses on earth of what I am about to do. I need my people to be familiar with my righteous purposes in bringing disasters, which will call the people of earth to awaken to My soon coming. I need each of you to cooperate with Me in My efforts to save every soul who is honest in heart. My people must be where I am in order for Me to accomplish what is necessary at this time. Like Noah, Abraham, and Lot, I need My people to preach My message and understand and uphold Me in what I am about to do.

Approximately two years passed by. Then on the evening of December 25, 2004, I was sitting in my office talking with a friend, who is a native of Malaysia. We were both sensing a strange ominous feeling of supernatural darkness. Recently, she had experienced a series of dreams where she saw a huge black wall of water coming toward her on the beach, people running for safety, and herself trying to help people to escape. Then she would be awakened by the sounds of her own screams of fear. We wondered if God had a message for her in allowing her to experience these dreams. Finally, she and her husband went home, and I went to bed.

Early in the morning, the phone rang. It was my friend! She was incoherent, sobbing and screaming into the phone. "Whatever is the matter? Please try to calm down and tell me!" I begged.

Finally she was able to gasp out the words, "There has been a terrible tsunami in my country, and I cannot locate my family!" I talked to her until she had calmed down. She was able to contact her family later in the afternoon. But now we knew that this was the meaning of the strange, frightening dreams. They were warnings of the series of disasters, which would begin the second of the seven trumpets!

Another tsunami hit on Easter 2005; then Hurricanes Katrina and Rita followed, rocking the world and making headlines, which questioned the meaning of the strange series of events. The few of us who knew that these disasters must be events marking the beginning of the second trumpet noticed that approximately three and a half years had elapsed since the falling of the towers. We wondered whether or not there was significance to this timing. Would it be repeated for the third trumpet? We could only wait and see.

The following texts are the ones that seemed most important to me in my study of the second trumpet:

> *The second angel sounded his trumpet,* and something like a huge mountain, all ablaze, was thrown into the sea. A third of the sea turned into blood, a third of the living creatures in the sea died, and a third of the ships were destroyed. (Rev. 8:8, 9, emphasis added)

> 'I am against you, you destroying mountain, you who destroy the whole earth,' declares the LORD. 'I will stretch out my hand against you, roll you off the cliffs, and make you a burned-out mountain.... *Lift up a banner in the land! Blow the trumpet among the nations!* (Jer. 51:25, 27; emphasis added)

> *All you people of the world, you who live on the earth, when a banner is raised on the mountains, you will see it, and when a trumpet sounds, you will hear it.* (Isa. 18:3, emphasis added)

> He who made the Pleiades and Orion ... who calls for the waters of the sea and pours them out over the face of the land—the LORD is his name. With a blinding flash, he destroys the stronghold and brings the fortified city to ruin. (Amos 5:8, 9)

> *When a trumpet sounds in a city, do not the people tremble? When disaster comes to a city, has not the LORD caused it?* Surely the Sovereign LORD does nothing without revealing his plan to his servants the prophets. The lion has roared—who will not fear? *The Sovereign LORD has spoken—who can but prophesy?* (Amos 3:6–8, emphasis added)

The Lord gives a special truth for the people in an emergency. Who dare refuse to publish it? He commands His servants to present the last invitation of mercy to the world. They cannot remain silent, except at the peril of their souls. Christ's ambassadors have nothing to do with consequences. They must perform their duty, and leave results with God. (*The Great Controversy*, pp. 609, 610)

'Prepare to meet thy God' is the message we are everywhere to proclaim. The trumpet is to give a certain sound. Clearly and distinctly the warning is to ring out: 'Babylon the great is fallen, is fallen.... Come out of her, My people, that ye be not partakers of her sins, and that ye receive not of her plagues.' Revelation 18:2–4. The words of this scripture are to be fulfilled. Soon the test is to come to all the inhabitants of the earth. At that time prompt decisions will be made. (*Testimonies for the Church*, vol. 9, p. 149, emphasis added)

The LORD will cause people to hear his majestic voice and will make them see his arm coming down with raging anger and consuming fire, with cloudburst, thunderstorm and hail. (Isa. 30:30, emphasis added)

God is speaking to us in these last days. We hear His voice in the storm, in the rolling thunder. We hear of the calamities He permits in the earthquakes the breaking forth of waters, and the destructive elements sweeping all before them.... God speaks to families who have refused to recognize Him, sometimes in the whirlwind and storm, sometimes face to face.... When the still small voice which succeeds the whirlwind and the tempest ... is heard, let all cover their face, for God is very near. (*Selected Messages*, vol. 2, pp. 315, 316, emphasis added)

Already the judgments of God are abroad in the land, as seen in storms, in floods, in tempests, in earthquakes, in peril by land and by sea. *The great I AM is speaking to those who make void His law. When God's wrath is poured out upon the earth, who will then be able to stand?* (*Testimonies for the Church*, vol. 5, p. 136, emphasis added)

There is no faithfulness, no love, no acknowledgment of God in the land. There is only cursing, lying and murder, stealing and adultery; they break all bounds, and bloodshed follows bloodshed. Because of this the land dries up, and all who live in it waste away; the beasts of the field, the birds in the sky and the fish in the sea are swept away. (Hos. 4:1–3)

> God's message for the inhabitants of earth today is, 'Be ye also ready: for in such an hour as ye think not the Son of Man cometh....' The conditions prevailing in society, and especially in the great cities of the nations, proclaim in thunder tones that the hour of God's judgment is come and that the end of all things earthly is at hand. We are standing on the threshold of the crisis of the ages. In quick succession the judgments of God will follow one another—fire, and flood, and earthquake, with war and bloodshed. *We are not to be surprised at this time by events both great and decisive; for the angel of mercy cannot remain much longer to shelter the impenitent.* (*Prophets and Kings*, p. 278, emphasis added)

My conclusion is that when God's Spirit is being withdrawn from the earth, natural disasters will greatly increase. When we see these things taking place, we must add our voices to the testimonies in nature that Jesus is coming soon.

#3. The Fall of America

> *The third angel sounded his trumpet,* and a great star, blazing like a torch, fell from the sky on a third of the rivers and on the springs of water—the name of the star is Wormwood. A third of the waters turned bitter, and many people died from the waters that had become bitter. (Rev. 8:10, 11, emphasis added).

As I studied the falling star of the third trumpet, I noticed that it was "falling" but not yet fallen, and that it was blazing brightly as it went down. In Scripture, "star" represents leadership (Rev. 1:20; Dan. 12:3). As I prayed for enlightenment, I felt impressed that the falling star would be America. For many years America has been the leading nation in the world because it was founded upon Biblical principles. But like all other nations who have lost their leadership position, America, also, is dependent upon its relationship to the truths of God's Word, if she is to retain the blessings of heaven. The following Scriptures point out what happens to a nation or people who do not continue in the pathway of obedience to God and His laws:

> The LORD said, 'It is because they have forsaken my law, which I set before them; they have not obeyed me or followed my law. Instead, they have followed the stubbornness of their hearts; they have followed the Baals as their ancestors taught them.'

Therefore, this is what the LORD Almighty, the God of Israel, says: 'See, I will make this people eat bitter food and drink poisoned water. (Jer. 9:13–15)

The prophets follow an evil course and use their power unjustly. 'Both prophet and priest are godless; even in my temple I find their wickedness,' declares the LORD. 'Therefore their path will become slippery; they will be banished to darkness and there they will fall…. I will make them eat bitter food and drink poisoned water because from the prophets of Jerusalem ungodliness has spread throughout the land.' (Jer. 23:10–15)

Make sure there is no man or woman, clan or tribe among you today whose heart turns away from the LORD our God to go and worship the gods of those nations; make sure there is no root among you that produces such bitter poison. (Deut. 29:18)

'You profane and wicked prince of Israel, whose day has come, whose time of punishment has reached its climax, this is what the Sovereign LORD says: Take off the turban, remove the crown. It will not be as it was. The lowly will be exalted and the exalted will be brought low. A ruin! A ruin! I will make it a ruin! The crown will not be restored until he to whom it rightfully belongs shall come; to him I will give it.' (Ezek. 21:25–27)

Ellen White makes some interesting comments on this subject as well:

The crown removed from Israel passed successively to the kingdoms of Babylon, Medo-Persia, Greece, and Rome. God says, 'It shall be no more, until He come whose right it is; and I will give it Him. (*Education*, p. 179)

To every nation and to every individual of today God has assigned a place in His great plan. Today men and nations are being measured by the plummet in the hand of Him who makes no mistake. All are by their own choice deciding their destiny, and God is overruling all for the accomplishment of His purposes. (*Education*, p. 178)

God gives nations a certain time of probation. He sends light and evidence, that, if received, will save them, but if refused as the Jews refused light, indignation and punishment will fall upon them. (*The Seventh-day Adventist Bible Commentary*, vol. 4, p. 1143)

In Revelation 13:11–14, a nation depicted as a lamb-like beast comes up from the earth. In prophetic language the word "beast" is symbolic of a nation. This nation at first displays the gentle characteristics of a lamb but eventually speaks like a dragon. As Seventh-day Adventists, we believe that this prophecy depicts the rise of America, which arose from the land, rather than coming from the sea, which is characteristic of nations that arise from conquests of war. And why does this lamb-like nation begin to speak like a dragon? Because in the prophecy, there is another world power which begins to change the course of their beliefs and lead them away from the God of their forefathers.

> It [the lamb-like beast] exercised all the authority of the first beast on its behalf, and made the earth and its inhabitants worship *the first beast, whose fatal wound had been healed*.... The second beast was given power to give breath to the image of the first beast, so that the image could speak and cause all who refused to worship the image to be killed. It also forced all people, great and small, rich and poor, free and slave, to receive a mark on their right hand or on their foreheads, so that they could not buy or sell unless they had the mark. (Rev. 13:12–17; emphasis added).

Who is this first beast whose fatal wound had been healed? The answer to this is found earlier in the chapter:

> And I saw a beast coming out of the sea. It had ten horns and seven heads ... and on each head a blasphemous name.... *One of the heads of the beast seemed to have a fatal wound, but the fatal wound had been healed*. The whole world was filled with wonder and followed the beast.... All inhabitants of the earth will worship the beast—all whose names have not been written in the Lamb's book of life, the Lamb who was slain from the creation of the world. (Rev. 13:1–8, emphasis added)

The information given in these texts is very important as we go into a deeper study of remaining trumpets, for they describe the continuing saga of the fall of America.

3 The Descent Begins

It was Sabbath morning, September 13, 2008. My husband was sick, and because I had tended to his needs before leaving for the little church next door, I was a bit late. As I walked to church, I felt strangely pensive, as if something was about to happen. I thought perhaps my feelings were in response to my concern about my husband's illness. I stepped through the door and quietly took my place in the Sabbath School class, which was already in progress. Soon I felt a Presence beside me, and a quiet voice spoke to my mind. "The descent has begun," He said. "Do not be afraid, for I will be with you and hold your hand."

Throughout the church service, I felt Him there. Several others mentioned that they also felt the presence of the Lord in the room. I said nothing about what I was experiencing, for I did not want to break the holiness of the communion between my soul and Jesus. I still wondered what could be so important that He would visit me, and what He meant by "the descent has begun." After the service was over, and I was walking back to my home, the sense of His presence gradually dissipated, and I felt normal again. Only then did I share my experience with the others, and we discussed the possible meaning of the message He had brought. We all marveled at the gracious visitation of our Lord's presence to our little congregation. It reminded us of some quotations from Ellen White:

> Think you not that Christ values those who live wholly for Him? Think you not that He visits those who, like the beloved John, are for His sake in hard and trying places? He finds His faithful ones, and holds communion with them, encouraging and strengthening them. (*This Day With God*, p. 159)

> There have been times when the blessing of God has been bestowed in answer to prayer, so that when others have come into the room, no sooner did they step over the threshold than

they exclaimed, 'The Lord is here!' Not a word had been uttered, but the blessed influence of God's holy presence was sensibly felt. The joy that comes from Jesus Christ was there; and in this sense the Lord had been in the room just as verily as He walked through the streets of Jerusalem, or appeared to the disciples when they were in the upper chamber, and said, 'Peace be unto you.' (*My Life Today*, p. 51)

Early the next day, a friend called and informed me that the stock market had fallen, and that some large companies such as Fannie Mae and Freddie Mac had gone down. So *this* was the meaning of the message, "The descent has begun"! It was three and a half years from the cluster of devastating disasters of the second trumpet, and the third trumpet was now beginning to sound. My mind went back to October 19, 1987, Black Monday, when the stock market fell. At that time I had asked the Lord, "Is this *it*—the beginning of the economic collapse that will bring on the time of trouble?" The impression came back, "No, but it is a warning of what is to come."

Ten years later on October 31, 1997, the Lord impressed me in my morning worship to call my friends and request that they fast and pray all day because the cup of wickedness was so full. I felt impressed that if His people did not pray, He would have to let the economy go down. I did as He asked me to do, and friends across the United States prayed and fasted with me. The stock market plunged all day in a free fall. And then, just minutes before it closed for the day, it turned and came up again, surprising everyone. I still have the newspaper article from the Washington Post:

STOCKS SURGE, BUT CAUSE IS UNCLEAR
LATEST STOCK MARKET SURGE LEAVES ANALYSTS BEWILDERED

New York, Nov. 3—Wall Street was happy today, but wasn't quite sure why as the Dow Jones industrial average soared 232.31 points.... Some market analysts and economists were happy to embrace the market's old optimism, while others scratched their heads and searched for an explanation.... 'For some reason, the market's happy,' said Mickey Levy, an economist at Nations Bank Montgomery Securities here. But there's no way you can ascribe today's strong stock market performance to economic factors.'

This is an example of how God is in ultimate control of our world in every minute detail, but the godly lives and prayers of His people are still incredibly important. As Revelation 7:1–3 makes clear, God is holding back the winds of strife until His chosen ones are sealed and ready for what is coming upon the world.

> Another angel, ascending from the east, cried to them, saying: 'Hurt not the earth, neither the sea, nor the trees, till we have sealed the servants of our God in their foreheads.' This points out the work we have now to do. A vast responsibility is devolving upon men and women of prayer throughout the land to petition that God will sweep back the cloud of evil and give a few more years of grace in which to work for the Master. Let us cry to God that the angels may hold the four winds until missionaries shall be sent to all parts of the world and shall proclaim the warning against disobeying the law of Jehovah. (*Testimonies for the Church*, vol. 5, pp. 717, 718)

Why, then, did God permit the economic drop in the fall of 2008? Perhaps one clue can be gathered from some things that happened earlier in that year. In the spring of 2008, Pope Benedict visited the United States and was given a royal welcome. Later it was reported that when President Bush was asked, "What did you see when you looked into the eyes of the Pope?" he replied, "I saw God."

Bush's statement was not the first time he had spoken out about his admiration of the papacy. On April 7, 2006, he spoke at the third Annual National Catholic Prayer Breakfast, which met at the Washington Hilton Hotel in Washington, D.C. Here are some of his historic statements:

> Some people believe you cannot distinguish between right and wrong. The Catholic Church rejects such a pessimistic view of human nature and offers a vision of human freedom and dignity rooted in the same self-evident truths of America's founding.... Freedom is a gift from the Almighty because it is—and because it is universal, our Creator has written it into all nature. To maintain this freedom, societies need high moral standards. And the Catholic Church and its institutions play a vital role in helping our citizens acquire the character we need to live as free people.

On March 21, 2001, President Bush also said, "The best way to honor Pope John Paul II, truly one of the great men, is to take his teaching seriously; is to listen to his words and put his words and teachings into action here in America. This is a challenge we must accept."

As Seventh-day Adventists, we see this as evidence of the healing of the deadly wound given to the "first beast" whose power and authority will be restored, according to Revelation 13:3, 8. Ellen White also provides insight into this beast:

> *Was healed.* There was a gradual revival in papal life in the years following the revolution in France. The papacy suffered a new setback when in 1870 the Papal States were taken from it. A significant event occurred in 1929 when the Lateran Treaty restored temporal power to the pope, who was given the rule of Vatican City.... However, the prophet envisioned a much greater restoration. He saw the wound completely healed, as the Greek implies.... This is still future. Though the papacy receives homage from certain groups, vast populations show it no deference. But that is to change. The beast of v. 11 'causeth the earth and them which dwell therein to worship the first beast, whose deadly wound was healed. (*The Seventh-day Bible Commentary*, vol. 7, pp. 817, 818, emphasis added)

> The United States today continues to maintain the principles of freedom guaranteed in the Constitution. The manner in which a change in policy will be brought about is outlined in the present prophecy. The change comes in connection with the final crisis immediately preceding the time when 'the kingdoms of this world ... [have] become the kingdoms of our Lord, and of his Christ. (*The Seventh-day Bible Commentary*, vol. 7, p. 820)

God keeps a record of the nations, and when the measure of iniquity rises, God allows disasters to come. Because of the resurgence of this power in modern times, God permits cause and effect to occur. I believe that there is a correlation between the restoration of temporal power to the pope on February 11, 1929, and the fall of the stock market on October 24–29 of that same year, which affected not only our country but also the rest of the world. I also believe this gives us a clue as to the reason why the economy was allowed to go down in September 2008. When moral integrity and understanding of truth reach a certain low point beyond which God cannot allow humanity to go, He steps in and acts to maintain His truth and His law and defend His people. Here is a quotation that explains this principle:

> There will soon be a sudden change in God's dealing. The world in its perversity is being visited by casualties,—by floods, storms,

fires, earthquakes, famines, wars, and bloodshed. The Lord is slow to anger, and great in power; yet He will not at all acquit the wicked. 'The Lord hath His way in the whirlwind and in the storm, and the clouds are the dust of His feet.' O that men might understand the patience and longsuffering of God! He is putting under restraint His own attributes. His omnipotent power is under the control of Omnipotence. O that men would understand that God refuses to be wearied out with the world's perversity, and still holds out the hope of forgiveness even to the most undeserving! But His forbearance will not always continue. Who is prepared for the sudden change that will take place in God's dealing with sinful men? Who will be prepared to escape the punishment that will certainly fall upon transgressors? (*Fundamentals of Christian Education*, pp. 356, 357)

And have these things captured the attention of the world? Indeed they have! But how many know the meaning of the events that are transpiring? Certainly as Seventh-day Adventists, these things must be put in the context of prophesies that we have understood for generations to be warnings of the imminent return of Jesus. Here is a quotation taken from the Hope Channel Newsletter, *HopeLink*, August, 2009.

Dear Friend: The past decade has been traumatic. One crisis after another has assaulted our peace and security. First, it was the terrorist attacks on September 11, 2001. Then in 2005, the most devastating hurricane season in recorded history.... Most recently, financial institutions have collapsed, the stock market has crashed, and businesses are struggling to survive.... Our world is going through change of prophetic proportions. World leaders recognize something unusual is happening. Gordon Brown, the Prime Minister of the United Kingdom, recently said, 'Historians will look back and say this was no ordinary time but a defining moment: an unprecedented period of global change, and a time when one chapter ended and another began.'

4 Trumpets Then and Now

Before beginning the chapter on the fourth trumpet, I want to consider the issue that concerns many about the topic of last-day trumpets. Most scholars prefer to stay with the interpretation of the seven trumpets that has been espoused since the days of our early Advent pioneers. This interpretation is called the historic view. Briefly, here is a synopsis of the historic view, as referenced from *The Seventh-day Adventist Bible Commentary*, vol. 7, pp. 788-796:

The First Trumpet: Invasion of the Roman Empire by the Visigoths under Alaric. This was the first of the Teutonic incursions into the Roman Empire that played such an important part in its final downfall.

The Second Trumpet: The sea, with the life in it and upon it, is shown as the special object of this judgment. This has been seen as the depredations of the Vandals, who dominated the western Mediterranean with a navy of pirates, pillaging the coasts of Spain, Italy, and Greece, and preying upon Roman shipping.

The Third Trumpet: This has been interpreted as portraying the ravages of the Huns under the leadership of their king Attila in the fifth century. They raised havoc in various regions of the tottering Roman Empire. Attila died in AD 453, and the Huns disappeared from history almost immediately.

The Fourth Trumpet: The sun, moon, and stars have been interpreted to represent the great luminaries of the Western Roman government—its emperors, senators, and consuls. With the extinction of Western Rome, the last of its emperors ceased to reign.

The Fifth and Sixth Trumpet: Textual evidence favors the reading "an eagle" (p. 789). The eagle may be thought of as an omen of doom (see Matt. 24:28, KJV; Deut. 28:49; Hos. 8:1). This warning of doom is specifically for the unrighteous inhabitants of earth. The fallen star occurs in Jewish apocalyptic literature to describe Satan as a star fallen from heaven. A number of commentators have identified the fifth and sixth trumpets with the ravages of the Saracens and the Turks, thus preparing the way for the Muslim conquests.

Some have suggested that inasmuch as the keeping of the Sabbath is ultimately to be the outward sign of the inner work of sealing by the Holy Spirit, the ones attacked by the "locusts" here are those who do not observe the true Sabbath.

Some who apply the fifth and sixth trumpets to the Muslim Arabs and Turks see in this king (Rev. 9:11) a reference to Osman, the traditional founder of the Ottoman Empire. Most commentators who interpret the fifth trumpet as applying to the Saracens have seen the Turks in the sixth.

The Seventh Trumpet: The seventh angel (Rev. 11:15) marks the beginning of the third woe. Seventh-day Adventists date its beginning as 1844 (pp. 804–806), when Jesus moved into the second apartment of the heavenly sanctuary and began the work of judgment. This is where He takes back the kingdoms of earth and prepares to reign forever and ever.

For many, the historic view, bringing us up to the preaching of the 1844 message, is satisfactory. It is no doubt true that if that generation had been ready to go forward, they could have lived to see the culmination of earth's history in their day.

> Had Adventists after the great disappointment in 1844 held fast their faith and followed on unitedly in the opening providence of God, receiving the message of the third angel and in the power of the Holy Spirit proclaiming it to the world, they would have seen the salvation of God, the Lord would have wrought mightily with their efforts, the work would have been completed, and Christ would have come ere this to receive His people to their reward.... It was not the will of God that the coming of Christ should be thus delayed.... We may have to remain here in this world because of insubordination many more years, as did the children of Israel; but for Christ's sake, His people should not add sin to sin by charging God with the consequence of their own wrong course of action. (*Evangelism*, pp. 695, 696)

Inspiration tells us that because of God's tender mercy and longsuffering, there has been a delay in His coming. In the meantime several more generations have come and gone. Are we to expect this to go on for even more generations before Jesus can come? Hopefully not! But how can we know when the day is truly approaching?

I believe God is answering this question by allowing a short, rapid repeat of the main points of the historic view for our generation, so that we have no excuse to delay His coming in our minds and put off our preparation until it is too late. The cry on that day will be bitter, as people finally realize that there is no second chance to get to know Jesus personally. As it was when the door to Noah's ark was closed, the still, small voice of the Holy Spirit will have withdrawn from all who refused to heed His tender call to repent.

> Then they will cry out to the LORD, but he will not answer them. At that time he will hide his face from them because of the evil they have done. This is what the LORD says, 'As for the prophets who lead my people astray, if one feeds them, they proclaim 'peace' if they have something to eat, but prepare to wage war against anyone who refuses to feed them. Therefore night will come over you, without visions, and darkness, without divination. The sun will set for the prophets, and the day will go dark for them. The seers will be ashamed and the diviners disgraced. They will all cover their faces because there is no answer from God.' (Micah 3:4–7)

What will bring about such spiritual darkness as is described here? The fourth trumpet predicts darkness upon a third of the sun, a third of the moon, and a third of the stars. As we noted in the historic view of the trumpets, this referred to the leaders of the Roman government in the last stages of their power. In prophetic history the Roman power was symbolized as the fourth beast to rule upon the earth, and was described in Daniel 7:7 as being "terrifying and frightening and very powerful…. It was different from all the former beasts, and it had ten horns."

As we look back in history, we find that when the Roman Empire came to an end, the nation broke up into ten tribes, which eventually became the kingdoms of Europe. But we are not finished with Rome, as the continuing prophecy reveals: "While I was thinking about the horns, there before me was *another horn*, a little one, which came up among them; and three of the first horns were uprooted before it. *This horn had eyes like the eyes of a human being and a mouth that spoke boastfully*" (Dan. 7:8, emphasis added). Who is this boastful little horn power? Again, history reveals the answer.

Ellen White tells us in *The Seventh-day Adventist Bible Commentary*, vol. 4, "'Out of the ruins of political Rome, arose the great moral Empire in the 'giant form' of the Roman Church.' (A. C. Flick, *The Rise of the Medieval Church* [1900], p. 150)" (p. 826). What are some of the boastful words that help to further identify this religious and political power? Note the following quotes: "All names which in the Scriptures are applied to Christ ... all the same names are applied to the Pope" (*On the Authority of Councils*, book 2) and "We hold upon this earth the place of God almighty" (*The Great Encyclical Letters of Leo*, XIII, p. 304).

In Daniel 7:21, this power was prophesied to wage war against the saints of God. It says, "As I watched, this horn was waging war against the holy people and defeating them." As a result of this persecution, it is estimated that up to 50 million people were killed during the six centuries of papal Inquisition (Amazing Discoveries, http://amazingdiscoveries.org, [accessed September 22, 2015]). The reign of the papacy ended when the pope was taken captive in 1798 by the French army and died in exile (see *The Great Controversy*, p. 266).

It is clear in Scripture that the little horn power, or papacy, will have a resurgence in the last days, with the help of the lamb-like beast, or America. This has always been accepted Seventh-day Adventist doctrine, based especially upon Revelation 13. Our forefathers understood that they were to "prophesy again" after the great disappointment in 1844 (Rev. 10:10, 11). But what were they to prophesy? Certainly not a specific date for the coming of Jesus, for we are not to know the day or the hour of His coming. But that does not mean that God will leave us without specific warnings and signs to know when His coming is near! One of the signs of Jesus' soon coming is the resurgence of the little horn power.

Revelation 13:3 says, "One of the heads of the beast seemed to have had a fatal wound, but the fatal wound had been healed. The whole world was filled with wonder and followed the beast." This is just one of the signs that are rapidly fulfilling in our day, but it is an important one, as we shall see in the following chapters of this book. In combination with all the other signs contained within the seven trumpet messages, there should be no doubt that Jesus' coming is imminent. Are people beginning to recognize these signs? Here are a few such indications:

> The tide began to turn when after 9/11 many began to question if the attack was a form of judgment from God. (*Inside Report* (Amazing Facts Newsletter), Spring, 2006.

> Lincoln [Steed, *Liberty* mag. editor] sees current world events as both fearsome and exciting. 'We're living in incredible times,' he says. 'I believe that just before 9/11 major religious issues were already bubbling up, but when 9/11 happened, everything hit the fan…! A hundred years ago there was a clear movement

to make the United States a 'Christian Nation,' and they had Sunday 'Blue Laws,' too. But what is different now is that all the problems we face lead up to a 'ground-zero' argument. They're converging so quickly that is seems impossible to go much further before the final events that are predicted in the Bible are upon us.' (*3ABN World*, July 2009)

Bill Wilson, an internationally syndicated Christian communicator, riddled a speech Tuesday with references to the second coming of Christ—an event he said would occur 'within years, not decades.' Wilson spoke to about 60 people at Otterbein United Brethren Church of Christ's Ministry Center. His remarks centered on what he said were the relationships between current world events and Bible prophecies that prove the world is living in the time immediately prior to the tribulation, a time to warn God's people to awaken and prepare themselves for Christ's imminent return. 'Signs point to a changing world', he said, 'to the end of time. This generation will see the return of Jesus. Something is about to happen.' (*The Waynesboro Herald*, Waynesboro, PA, by Richard F. Belisle. Sept. 29, 2004.

There is a fight for the destiny of the USA right now. The destiny of America hangs in the balance. The Lord is calling His people to arise and pray for the United States of America. It is time to contend. (Breaking Christian News, http://www.breakingchristiannews.com, [accessed September 23, 2015])

Barring a miracle, the family that has existed since antiquity will likely crumble, presaging the fall of Western civilization itself. This is a time for concerted prayer, divine wisdom and greater courage than we have ever been called upon to exercise. (WorldNetDaily, www.wnd.com, [accessed September 23, 2015]).

Are we to sit idly by, waiting for something *really* big to happen before we venture to warn others that probationary time is running out? God forbid that we should fail God at this precipitous time in earth's history!

Put the trumpet to your lips! An eagle is over the house of the LORD because the people have broken my covenant and rebelled against my law. (Hos. 8:1)

The days of punishment are coming, the days of reckoning are at hand. Let Israel know this. (Hos. 9:7)

The perils of the last days are upon us, and in our work we are to warn the people of the danger they are in. Let not the solemn scenes which prophecy has revealed be left untouched. If our people were half awake, if they realized the nearness of the events portrayed in the Revelation, a reformation would be wrought in our churches, and many more would believe the message. (*Evangelism*, p. 195)

Blow the trumpet in Zion; sound an alarm in the holy mountain. Gather the host of the Lord, with sanctified hearts, to hear what the Lord will say unto His people; for *He has increased light for all who will hear*. Let them be armed and equipped, and come up to the battle—to the help of the Lord against the mighty. (*Testimonies to Ministers and Gospel Workers*, p. 410, emphasis added)

The voice of the true watchman needs now to be heard all along the line, 'The morning cometh, and also the night....' The trumpet must give a certain sound, for we are in the great day of the Lord's preparation. (*Selected Messages*, vol. 2, p. 379)

But what correlation is there between the seven trumpets of Revelation and the need for urgency in preaching the nearness of Jesus' coming? Notice carefully this quotation from Ellen White:

The seven angels stood before God to receive their commission. To them were given seven trumpets. The Lord was going forth to punish the inhabitants of the earth for their iniquity, and the earth was to disclose her blood and no more cover her slain. (*Manuscript Releases*, vol. 15, p. 219)

This quotation combines the message and purpose of the seven trumpets with Isaiah 26:

Come, my people, enter thou into thy chambers, and shut thy doors about thee: hide thyself as it were for a little moment, *until the indignation be overpast*. For, behold, the LORD cometh out of his place to punish the inhabitants of the earth for their iniquity:

the earth also shall disclose her blood, and shall no more cover her slain (verses 20, 21, KJV, emphasis added)

God's final 'indignation' takes the form of what is known as the seven last plagues (Rev. 14:10; 15:1, etc.).... *During the seven last plagues God invites His people to make Him their hiding place, that He may be to them a 'refuge and strength, a very present help in trouble' (Ps. 46:1).'* (*The Seventh-day Adventist Bible Commentary,* vol. 4, pp. 204, 205, emphasis added)

In every case where Ellen White quotes this phrase, it always indicates the seven last plagues. Here are only a few:

The conditions prevailing in society, and especially in the great cities of the nations, proclaim in thunder tones that the hour of God's judgment is come and that the end of all things earthly is at hand. We are standing on the threshold of the crisis of the ages. In quick succession the judgments of God will follow one another—fire, and flood, and earthquake, with war and bloodshed. We are not to be surprised at this time by events both great and decisive; for the angel of mercy cannot remain much longer to shelter the impenitent. 'Behold, the Lord cometh out of His place to punish the inhabitants of the earth for their iniquity: the earth also shall disclose her blood, and shall no more cover her slain....' The storm of God's wrath is gathering.... The righteous alone shall be hid with Christ in God till the desolation be overpast. (*Prophets and Kings,* p. 278)

The wickedness of the inhabitants of the world has almost filled up the measure of their iniquity. This earth has almost reached the place where God will permit the destroyer to work his will upon it. The substitution of the laws of men for the law of God, *the exaltation ... of Sunday in place of the Bible Sabbath, is the last act in the drama. When this substitution becomes universal, God will reveal Himself. He will arise in His majesty to shake terribly the earth.* He will come out of His place to punish the inhabitants of the world for their iniquity, and the earth shall disclose her blood and shall no more cover her slain. (*Testimonies for the Church,* vol. 7, p. 141, emphasis added)

There are hypocrites now who will tremble when they obtain a view of themselves. Their own vileness will terrify them in that day which is soon to come upon us, a day when 'the Lord cometh out of His place to punish the inhabitants of the earth for their iniquity.' (*Testimonies for the Church*, vol. 2, p. 446)

Because of the obvious correlation between the seven trumpets and the seven last plagues, some students of prophecy have equated them to be one and the same. But trumpets in the Bible and Spirit of Prophecy are always used as warnings of what is about to come, whether it is war, disasters, or some imminent danger, which gives the hearers of the trumpet message time to prepare, or escape before it is too late. Isaiah 26:20 is just such a message, and correlates perfectly with God's final call to the world, which is found in Revelation 18:

Come out of her, my people, so that you will not share in her sins, so that you will not receive any of her plagues; for her sins are piled up to heaven, and God has remembered her crimes. (verses 4, 5, emphasis added)

'The end of all things is at hand.' 1 Peter 4:7. 'Prepare to meet thy God' is the message we are everywhere to proclaim. *The trumpet is to give a certain sound. Clearly and distinctly the warning is to ring out: 'Babylon the great is fallen, is fallen..... Come out of her, My people, that ye be not partakers of her sins, and that ye receive not of her plagues.'* Revelation 18:2–4.The words of this scripture are to be fulfilled. Soon the last test is to come to all the inhabitants of the earth. (*Testimonies for the Church*, vol. 9, p. 149, emphasis added)

Notice how the blowing of the trumpet is associated with the final warning given by God's people to earth's inhabitants, who are facing the seven last plagues. But first we must hear the sound of the trumpets ourselves and rightly interpret their meaning!

When the watchman, seeing the sword coming, gives the trumpet a certain sound ... all will have opportunity to make ready for the conflict. But too often the leader has stood hesitating.... The very hesitancy and uncertainty on his part is crying: "'Peace and safety.' Do not get excited. Be not alarmed...." Thus he virtually denies the message sent from God, and the warning which was designed to stir the churches fails to do its work. The trumpet of the watchman gives no certain sound, and the people do not prepare for the battle. Let the watchman beware lest, through his hesitancy and delay, souls shall be left to perish, and their blood shall be required at his hand. (*Testimonies for the Church*, vol. 5, pp. 715, 716)

All trumpet messages are to focus the attention of the people of earth on one climactic event—the second coming of Jesus.

Then the angel I had seen standing on the sea and on the land raised his right hand to heaven ... and said, 'There will be no more delay! But *in the days when the seventh angel is about to sound his trumpet, the mystery of God will be accomplished*, just as he announced to his servants the prophets.' (Rev. 10:5–7, emphasis added)

Then will appear the sign of the Son of Man in heaven. And then all the peoples of the earth will mourn when they see the Son of Man coming on the clouds of heaven, with power and great glory. And *he will send his angels with a loud trumpet call*, and they will gather his elect from the four winds, from one end of the heavens to the other. Now learn this lesson from the fig tree: As soon as its twigs get tender and its leaves come out, you know that summer is near. *Even so, when you see all these things, you know that it is near, right at the door. Truly I tell you, this generation will certainly not pass away until all these things have happened.* Heaven and earth will pass away, but my words will never pass away" (Matt. 24:30–35, emphasis added)

It would seem from this text that although we will not know the day or hour of the second coming of Jesus, He wants His followers to know when it is near, even at the door. In fact, the implication of the text is that we *can* know when we are in the last generation that will not pass away before He comes. Just as we know the signs of the passing yearly seasons, so we are to interpret the signs of His second coming. These signs are to be seen in the world around us, but how many are alert to the signs that God is sending? This is why the understanding of the seven trumpets is so important to the people of God today.

5 The Final Generation

In this chapter I want to address the question, why do we need to have a repeat of the seven trumpets? The most obvious answer is because this generation is the one who will see the repeat of the little horn power. Because of this, every person will have to make their eternal decision based upon how they respond to the challenge of papal world dominance.

During the Dark Ages, up to 50 million followers of Christ died defending their faith against the dogmas of the Catholic Church, but that means little, if anything, to Christians today. Yet this is the generation who will be held responsible for their personal decisions in the last act of the drama. In God's mercy He provides repeated warnings of the coming judgments and gives people now the same opportunity to live for truth against error that the former generations have had. Notice this parallel for the Jewish people before the close of their probation as a nation and the destruction of Jerusalem.

> Woe to you, because you build tombs for the prophets, and it was your ancestors who killed them. So you testify that you approve of what your ancestors did; they killed the prophets, and you build their tombs. Because of this, God in His wisdom said, 'I will send them prophets and apostles, some of whom they will kill and others they will persecute.' Therefore this generation will be held responsible for the blood of all the prophets that has been shed since the beginning of the world, from the blood of Abel to the blood of Zechariah, who was killed between the altar and the sanctuary. Yes, I tell you, this generation will be held responsible for it all. (Luke 11:47–51)

Since our generation will be held responsible for allowing sin to reach the culmination of all previous ages, so they also will be given the full light of both the early and the latter rain during the preaching of the loud cry of

Revelation 18:4, 5: "Come out of her, my people, so that you will not share in her sins, so that you will not receive any of her plagues; for her sins are piled up to heaven, and God has remembered her crimes." This indicates that mystical Babylon, the harlot of Revelation 17, who "was drunk with the blood of God's holy people, the blood of those who bore testimony to Jesus" (verse 6) in the Dark Ages, will rise to power again. The cup of her iniquity will be filled in the final generation, when her sins will reach heaven and bring down God's final judgment upon her and all the wicked who follow her teachings (see Rev. 18:5, 6; Rev. 17:8, 11; Dan. 7:11, 26).

> The beast, which you saw, once was, now is not, and yet will come up out of the Abyss and go to its destruction. The inhabitants of the earth whose names have not been written in the book of life from the creation of the world will be astonished when they see the beast, because it once was, now is not, and yet will come....The beast who once was, and now is not, is an eighth king. He belongs to the seven and is going to his destruction.... They will wage war against the Lamb, but the Lamb will triumph over them because He is Lord of lords and King of kings—and with him will be his called, chosen and faithful followers.... The woman you saw is the great city that rules over the kings of the earth. (Rev. 17:8–18)

Since 1929, we have seen a reestablishment of the Papacy. "The state of Vatican City was constituted by the Lateran Treaty ... in 1929, which assured the Holy See absolute independence and guaranteed it sovereignty also in international relations" (*Encyclopedia Britannica*, vol. 22, p. 905, 1971 edition). Ellen White has insight into this as well. Look at what she says after quoting Revelation 18:

> This scripture points forward to a time when the announcement of the fall of Babylon, as made by the second angel of Revelation 14 (verse 8), is to be repeated, with the additional mention of the corruptions which have been entering the various organizations that constitute Babylon, since that message was first given, in the summer of 1844. A terrible condition of the religious world is here described. With every rejection of truth the minds of the people will become darker, their hearts more stubborn, until they are entrenched in an infidel hardihood. In defiance of the warnings which God has given, they will continue to trample upon one of the precepts of the Decalogue, until they are led to

persecute those who hold it sacred.... Of Babylon, at the time brought to view in this prophecy, it is declared: 'Her sins have reached unto heaven, and God hath remembered her iniquities.' Revelation 18:5. She has filled up the measure of her guilt, and destruction is about to fall upon her. (*The Great Controversy*, pp. 603, 604)

For the generation who reaches this climax of history, God will send warnings of the coming destruction. I believe the seven trumpets of Revelation depict such warnings. I see in the historical view of the trumpets a pattern of what is happening today. As Ellen White has said:

In the great final conflict, Satan will employ the same policy, manifest the same spirit, and work for the same end as in all preceding ages. That which has been, will be, except that the coming struggle will be marked with a terrible intensity such as the world has never witnessed. (*The Great Controversy*, p. xi)

Each of the ancient prophets spoke less of their own time than for ours, so that their prophesying is in force for us.... The Bible has accumulated and bound up together its treasures for this last generation. (*Selected Messages*, vol. 3, pp. 338, 339)

In the historic view of the trumpets, the first trumpet, Alaric, leader of the Visigoths, made the first incursion into the Roman Empire. It took four stages to take Rome down. The fifth and sixth trumpets represent the attacks of the Muslim hoards over Europe.

The second woe is ... the shameful Mohammed Church—with their doctrines and with the sword. (*Luther's Works*, Muhlenberg, 1932, VI:482f)

The Turk again prepares to wage war with a larger force, who will stand up to oppose his marching throughout the length and breadth of the land at his mere will and pleasure? (*Selected Works of John Calvin: Tracts and Letters*, pp. 373–375)

One of the first Biblical expositors on record to identify the Turks as the power portrayed under the sixth trumpet was the Swiss reformer, Heinrich Bullinger (d. A.D. 1575), although Martin

Luther had already set forth this trumpet as symbolic of Moslems. (*The Seventh-day Adventist Bible Commentary*, vol. 7, p. 794)

In *The Great Controversy* pages 334, 335, Ellen G. White commends the work of Josiah Litch, who studied the time prophecy in the fifth trumpet, and a few days before its accomplishment predicted the fall of the Ottoman Empire on the 11th of August 1840. As far as we know, the only recognition of the historic view of the prophecies in Revelation 8 and 9 at the actual time of their fulfillment was of the sixth trumpet in the Dark Ages, and the fifth trumpet in 1840, and these are not in their natural order. The others were extrapolated by looking back into past history. The historic trumpets, then, can be seen as patterns from the past to guide us in our recognition of the final trumpet warnings to the last generation. Prophecies are meant to be recognized when the time comes for them to be fulfilled.

> I am telling you now before it happens, so that when it does happen you will believe. (John 13:19; also see John 14:29)

> I have told you this, so that when the time comes you will remember.... But when he, the Spirit of truth, comes, he will guide you into all truth.... And he will tell you what is yet to come. (John 16:4, 13)

> See, the former things have taken place, and new things I declare; before they spring into being I announce them to you. (Isa. 42:9)

Prophecies are obscure until the generation to whom they apply recognizes their fulfillment through the revelation of the Holy Spirit. This was certainly true of the pioneers of the Adventist church. The recognition that they were the people represented in Revelation 10:9, 10 gave them the courage and dedication that carried them through the disappointment of 1844. They knew they were the chosen ones to whom God was entrusting the message of the sanctuary, the investigative judgment, and the assurance of His soon coming.

This was also true in Jesus' day. In spite of centuries of anticipating the coming of the Messiah, very few recognized Him. The prophecies had been so misconstrued to suit the desires of the teachers of the Scriptures that only the ones with open hearts could hear the still, small voice of the Holy Spirit. Zacharias and Elizabeth, Joseph and Mary, the shepherds, the wise men—how few were listening to the heavenly messengers who were waiting to spread the good news of the Messiah!

Outside of the Jewish nation there were men who foretold the appearance of a divine instructor. These men were seeking for truth, and to them the Spirit of Inspiration was imparted. One after another, like stars in the darkened heavens, such teachers had arisen. Their words of prophecy had kindled hope in the hearts of thousands of the Gentile world.... Among those whom the Jews styled heathen were men who had a better understanding of the Scripture prophecies concerning the Messiah than had the teachers in Israel. There were some who hoped for His coming as a deliverer from sin. (*The Desire of Ages*, p. 33)

Had the leaders in Israel been true to their trust, they might have shared the joy of heralding the birth of Jesus. But now they are passed by. God declares, 'I will pour water upon him that is thirsty, and floods upon the dry ground.' 'Unto the upright there ariseth light in the darkness.' Isaiah 44:3; Psalm 112:4. To those who are seeking for light, and who accept it with gladness, the bright rays from the throne of God will shine. (*The Desire of Ages,* p. 47)

So it is in every age. It is neither the mighty nor the great who are destined to recognize a prophecy when its time has come. It is men and women of any station in life who are studying the Scriptures, praying for light, and are open to the leading of the Holy Spirit. Daniel is a shining example of such a man:

I, Daniel, understood from the Scriptures, according to the word of the LORD given to Jeremiah the prophet, that the desolation of Jerusalem would last seventy years. So I turned to the Lord God and pleaded with him in prayer and petition, in fasting, and in sackcloth and ashes.... While I was speaking and praying, confessing my sin and the sin of my people Israel and making my request to the LORD my God for His holy hill—while I was still in prayer, Gabriel ... came to me in swift flight about the time of the evening sacrifice. He instructed me and said to me, 'Daniel, I have now come to give you insight and understanding. As soon as you began to pray, a word went out, which I have come to tell you, for you are highly esteemed. (Dan. 9:2, 3, 20–23)

Wouldn't we all like to hear the commendation of heaven that was given to Daniel? And we can, if we are as diligent and prayerful as he was.

Notice that an answer was given as soon as he began to pray. Who do you suppose gave that answer to Daniel? Surely it was from the throne in heaven, possibly from the Father to His Son in His preexistent position as Michael the Archangel, leader of the angels (see Rev. 12:7). Even now, Jesus hears the cry of the weakest saint who is pleading for light and understanding. Just as He appeared to His followers after His resurrection to help them understand His mission on earth, so He will respond to us when we cry for help to know the meaning of the signs of our times!

> He said to them, 'How foolish you are, and how slow of heart to believe all that the prophets have spoken...! And beginning with Moses and all the Prophets, he explained to them what was said in all the Scriptures concerning himself. (Luke 24:25, 27)

> He said to them, 'This is what I told you while I was still with you: Everything must be fulfilled that is written about me in the Law of Moses, the Prophets and the Psalms.' Then he opened their minds so they could understand the Scriptures. (Luke 24: 44, 45)

I want my mind opened so I can understand the Scriptures, don't you? As the Psalmist says, "Open my eyes that I may see wonderful things in your law" (Ps. 119:18).

6 God's Majestic Voice

The young man seated in front of me looked straight into my eyes. "God is coming!" he said, abruptly. His bold statement surprised me.

"What makes you say that?" I asked.

"Because of all the things that are happening in the world," he replied. "It all started with 9/11 when the towers fell. And then the tsunamis and hurricanes, and birds falling out of the sky, and thousands of fish dying for no reason, and strange voices in the sky! It all means that God is coming!"

I could hardly believe what I was hearing. This 14-year-old was not a person one would generally expect to hear such statements coming from his mouth. I had been counseling him for several weeks about a school problem. His mother randomly called me one day after finding my name online. I visited their home—a trailer on a barren hillside in the back woods of West Virginia, several miles from my home.

His story was one of poverty, shifted from home to home since early childhood, and family problems. He had not attended school for three years, but now his mother had taken him back, and wanted to make up for past neglect. He was obviously very intelligent, in spite of his deprived childhood. He had been taken to church by his grandmother at some point in his life but was not attending any church at that time.

"How do you know about these things?" I asked.

"I read them in the newspaper," he said. "And I know that the world is coming to an end and God is coming."

I am happy to report that shortly after this conversation, he gave his heart to Jesus, and both he and his mother are planning to attend our church. I am still amazed at the lesson this has taught me—that God is speaking through the trumpets to many people who would otherwise have no chance to get ready for Jesus to come. It has also taught me that God is no respecter of persons. He will speak to anyone who has spiritual ears to hear and perceive what He is saying by the "majestic voice" of the trumpets.

> The LORD will cause people to hear his majestic voice, and will make them see his arm coming down with raging anger and consuming fire, with cloudburst, thunderstorm and hail. (Isa. 30:30)

> God is speaking to us in these last days. We hear His voice in the storm, in the rolling thunder. We hear of the calamities He permits in the earthquakes, the breaking forth of waters, and the destructive elements sweeping all before them.... God speaks to families who have refused to recognize Him, sometimes in the whirlwind and storm, sometimes face to face as He talked with Moses.... When the still small voice which succeeds the whirlwind and the tempest ... is heard, let all cover their face, for God is very near. Let them hide themselves in Jesus Christ; for He is their hiding place. (*Selected Messages*, vol. 2, pp. 315, 316)

> Already the judgments of God are abroad in the land, as seen in storms, in floods, in tempests, in earthquakes, in peril by land and by sea. The great I AM is speaking to those who make void His law. When God's wrath is poured out upon the earth, who will then be able to stand? (*Testimonies for the Church*, vol. 5, p. 136)

Can you see now how the seven trumpets are representative of God's voice speaking to everyone who will listen before the outpouring of the seven last plagues? God wants His people to come into the refuge He provides.

Let's take a closer look now at the correlation between the trumpets and the seven plagues. First of all, the seven trumpets are all poured out upon *a third* of the earth, while the plagues are "the wrath of God, which is poured out *without mixture* into the cup of his indignation" (Rev. 14:10, KJV, emphasis added).

> God keeps a reckoning with the nations. Through every century of this world's history evil workers have been treasuring up wrath against the day of wrath; and when the time fully comes that iniquity shall have reached the stated boundary of God's mercy, His forbearance will cease. When the accumulated figures in heaven's record books shall mark the sum of transgression complete, wrath will come, unmixed with mercy, and then it will be seen what a tremendous thing it is to have worn out the divine patience. This crisis will be reached when the nations shall unite in making void God's law. (*Testimonies for the Church*, vol. 5, p. 524)

I believe that each trumpet is a limited warning of what will happen to the whole world at the coming of Jesus.

#1. Fall of towers are a warning of the total collapse of mystical Babylon, as well as all the cities of the world, at the second coming of Jesus.

> Take up your positions around Babylon.... for she has sinned against the LORD. Shout against her on every side! She surrenders, *her towers fall*, her walls are torn down. Since this is the vengeance of the LORD, take vengeance on her; do to her as she has done to others. (Jer. 50:14, 15, emphasis added)

> Give back to her as she has given; pay her back double for what she has done. Pour her a double portion from her own cup.... In one day her plagues will overtake her: death, mourning and famine. She will be consumed by fire, for mighty is the Lord God who judges her.... Woe! Woe to you, great city, you mighty city of Babylon! In one hour your doom has come! (Rev. 18:6–10)

> Their land is full of idols; they bow down to the work of their hands.... So people will be brought low and everyone humbled— do not forgive them. Go into the rocks, hide in the ground from the fearful presence of the LORD and the splendor of his majesty! The eyes of the arrogant will be humbled and human pride brought low; the LORD alone will be exalted in that day.... The Lord Almighty has a day in store for all the proud and lofty ... for all the towering mountains and all the high hills, for *every lofty tower* and every fortified wall, for every trading ship and every stately vessel. The arrogance of man will be brought low and human pride humbled; the LORD alone will be exalted in that day, and the idols will totally disappear. (Isa. 2:8–18, emphasis added)

> The great city split into three parts and *the cities of the nations collapsed*. God remembered Babylon the Great and gave her the cup filled with the wine of the fury of his wrath. (Rev. 16:19, emphasis added)

#2. Natural disasters are a warning of the complete breakup of nature at the coming of Christ.

The seventh angel poured out his bowl into the air, and out of the temple came a loud voice from the throne, saying, 'It is done!' Then there came flashes of lightning, rumblings, peals of thunder and a severe earthquake. No earthquake like it has ever occurred since mankind has been on the earth, so tremendous was the quake.... Every island fled away and the mountains could not be found. From the sky huge hailstones, each weighing about a hundred pounds, fell upon people. (Rev. 16:17–21)

I watched as he opened the sixth seal. There was a great earthquake. The sun turned black like sackcloth made of goat hair, the whole moon turned blood red, and the stars in the sky fell to earth, as figs drop from a fig tree when shaken by a strong wind. The heavens receded like a scroll being rolled up, and every mountain and island was removed from its place. (Rev. 6:12–14)

People will flee to caves in the rocks and to holes in the ground from the fearful presence of the LORD and the splendor of his majesty, when he rises to shake the earth.... They will flee to caverns in the rocks and to the overhanging crags from the fearful presence of the LORD and the splendor of his majesty, when he rises to shake the earth. (Isa. 2:19, 21; see Rev. 6:15–17)

It is at midnight that God manifests His power for the deliverance of His people. The sun appears, shining in its strength. Signs and wonders follow in quick succession.... Everything in nature seems turned out of its course. The streams cease to flow.... There is a mighty earthquake, 'such as was not since men were upon the earth....' The firmament appears to open and shut.... The mountains shake like a reed in the wind, and ragged rocks are scattered on every side. There is a roar as of a coming tempest. The sea is lashed into fury. There is heard the shriek of the hurricane.... The whole earth heaves and swells like the waves of the sea. Its surface is breaking up. Its very foundations seem to be giving way. Mountain chains are sinking. Inhabited islands disappear. The seaports ... are swallowed up by the angry waters. Babylon the great has come in remembrance before God, 'to give unto her the cup of the wine of the fierceness of His wrath.' (*The Great Controversy*, pp. 636, 637)

#3. The fall of the economy is a warning of the complete collapse of the world systems at the end of time.

> Wail, you who live in the market district; all your merchants will be wiped out, all who trade with silver will be destroyed. *At that time I will search Jerusalem with lamps and punish those who are complacent, who are like wine left on its dregs, who think, 'The LORD will do nothing, either good or bad.'* Their wealth will be plundered, their houses demolished. Though they build great houses, they will not live in them; though they will plant vineyards, they will not drink the wine. The great day of the LORD is near—near and coming quickly. The cry on the day of the LORD is bitter; the Mighty Warrior shouts his battle cry. That day will be a day of wrath—a day of distress and anguish, a day of trouble and ruin, a day of darkness and gloom, a day of clouds and blackness—*a day of trumpet and battle cry against the fortified cities and against the corner towers*.... Neither their silver nor their gold will be able to save them on the day of the LORD's wrath. In the fire of his jealousy the whole world will be consumed, for he will make a sudden end of all who live on the earth. (Zeph. 1:11–18, emphasis added)

Please notice that the time when the economy falls will be a time of judgment for God's professed followers who have put off the day of preparation. Trumpets are warnings of what is to come—warnings to get ready while there is still time! Therefore, He carefully warns His people to get ready and come into the hiding place *before* it is too late (see Isa. 26:20, 21; Rev. 18:4).

> Gather together, gather yourselves together, you shameful nation, *before the decree takes effect and that day passes like windblown chaff, before the LORD's fierce anger comes upon you, before the day of the LORD's wrath comes upon you.* Seek the LORD, all you humble of the land, you who do what he commands. Seek righteousness, seek humility; perhaps you will be sheltered on the day of the LORD's anger. (Zeph. 2:1–3, emphasis added)

Can we see more clearly now why Ellen White places the seven trumpets in direct correlation with the preparation of God's people to escape the seven last plagues? Let's read the quotation again:

> The seven angels stood before God to receive their commission. To them were given seven trumpets. The Lord was going forth to punish the inhabitants of the earth for their iniquity, and the earth was to disclose her blood and no more cover her slain. (*Manuscript Releases*, vol. 15, p. 219)

In this short statement is hidden the clue that the trumpets are directly connected with the preparation to escape the plagues. Some believe the trumpets and plagues are one and the same, but this cannot be. In Scripture, trumpets are always warnings to God's people to escape a danger that is imminent, and they give instructions about how to escape what is about to occur. As Paul says in 1 Corinthians 14:6, 8: "What good will I be to you, unless I bring you some revelation or knowledge or prophecy or word of instruction…? *Again, if the trumpet does not sound a clear call, who will get ready for battle?*" (emphasis added).

Trumpets have no purpose if everyone on planet Earth has already made their final decision. I think the confusion about the application of the seven trumpets has been that in spite of the numerous statements of Ellen White that the prophecies of Daniel and Revelation will be repeated for the final generation, we have not realized the necessity of these warnings to awaken everyone around the globe. Remember, prophecies are meant to be understood *when they happen*. For example, read the messianic prophecy in Zechariah 9:9: "Rejoice greatly, Daughter of Zion! Shout, Daughter of Jerusalem! See, your king comes to you, righteous and victorious, lowly and riding on a donkey, on a colt, the foal of a donkey."

We know what this prophecy means because we are looking back on its fulfillment. But when Jesus entered Jerusalem riding on a donkey, the people believed that this was the long-awaited king who would deliver them from the Romans. If we read this prophecy in the context of the verses that surround it, there is no question that this would be the most obvious interpretation. But God often gives prophecies that include greater time spans or inclusive meanings, which cover more than is apparent until the prophecy is actually fulfilled. Even then, we must be open to the Holy Spirit's guidance to connect the prophecy with the events that we are seeing, just as the disciples were dependent upon Jesus to explain the meaning of what they had experienced. "At first his disciples did not understand all this. Only after Jesus was glorified did they realize that these things had been written about him and that these things had been done to him" (John 12:16).

Today, as we see prophecy unfolding, we must be diligent students of the Word and have open hearts to hear what the Holy Spirit is speaking to us personally and to our generation. We must "give the trumpet a certain sound," which will help people understand where we are in time and what must be done to prepare for the coming of Jesus.

> If ever God's watchmen needed to be on their guard, it is now.... The trumpet must give a certain sound. There will be a general proclamation of truth, the whole earth will be enlightened with the glory of God, but those only will recognize the light who have sought to know the difference between holiness and sin. (*The Upward Look*, p. 365)

> The watchman is to know the time of night. (*Testimonies for the Church*, vol. 6, p. 407)

> The perils of the last days are upon us, and in our work we are to warn the people of the danger they are in.... If our people were half awake, if they realized the nearness of the events portrayed in the Revelation, a reformation would be wrought in our churches, and many more would believe the message. We have no time to lose; God calls upon us to watch for souls as they that must give an account. (*Testimonies to Ministers and Gospel Workers*, p. 118)

> The day God visits you has come, the day your watchmen sound the alarm. (Micah 7:4)

> I foretold the former things long ago, my mouth announced them and I made them known; then suddenly I acted, and they came to pass.... From the first announcement I have not spoken in secret; at the time it happens, I am there. (Isa. 48:3, 16)

Isn't it comforting to know that when things that are prophesied begin to come to pass, our God is right there with us? We do not need to be afraid of anything that is happening or that is about to happen. God is watching over us and will tenderly care for us. He will provide for our every need.

> When tempted to sin, let us remember that Jesus is pleading for us in the heavenly sanctuary. When we put away our sins and come to Him in faith, He takes our names on His lips, and presents them to His Father, saying, 'I have graven them upon the palms of my hands; I know them by name.' And the command

goes forth to the angels to protect them. (*The Seventh-day Adventist Bible Commentary*, vol. 4, p. 1143)

I saw that our bread and water will be sure at that time, and that we shall not lack or suffer hunger; for God is able to spread a table for us in the wilderness. (*Early Writings*, p. 56)

The fruit of righteousness will be peace; its effect will be quietness and confidence forever. My people will live in peaceful dwelling places, in secure homes, in undisturbed places of rest. Though hail flattens the forest and the city is leveled completely, how blessed you will be, sowing your seed by every stream, and letting your cattle and donkeys range free. (Isa. 32:17–20)

7 Who Has the Mark?

"The fourth angel sounded his trumpet, and a third of the sun was struck, a third of the moon, and a third of the stars, so that a third of them turned dark. A third of the day was without light, and also a third of the night" (Rev. 8:12, emphasis added).

In order to understand the fourth trumpet, we must go back to the third (see chapter 3 of this book), where the falling star named Wormwood fell upon the waters and made them bitter. Water here represents the flow of spiritual light coming from the heavenly sanctuary.

> The man brought me back to the entrance to the temple, and I saw water coming out from under the threshold of the temple toward the east.... Swarms of living creatures will live wherever the river flows.... *So where the river flows everything will live....* Fruit trees of all kinds will grow on both banks of the river. Their leaves will not wither, nor will their fruit fail ... *because the water from the sanctuary flows to them.* (Ezek. 47:1, 9, 12, emphasis added)

As the spiritual leaders in America follow the teachings of the papacy, and they join hands together, spiritual darkness will descend upon them, and they will experience the condition described in the following Scriptures:

> Make sure there is no man or woman, clan or tribe among you today whose heart turns away from the LORD our God to go and worship the gods of those nations; make sure there is no root among you that produces such bitter poison. (Deut. 29:18)

> The LORD said, 'It is because they have forsaken my law, which I set before them; they have not obeyed me or followed my law. Instead, they have followed the stubbornness of their hearts;

they have followed the Baals, as their ancestors taught them.' Therefore, this is what the LORD Almighty, the God of Israel, says: 'See, I will make this people eat bitter food and drink poisoned water.' (Jer. 9:13–15)

'The prophets follow an evil course and use their power unjustly. Both prophet and priest are godless; even in my temple I find their wickedness,' declares the LORD. 'Therefore their path will become slippery; *they will be banished to darkness and there they will fall*.... I will make them eat bitter food and drink poisoned water, because from the prophets of Jerusalem ungodliness has spread throughout the land.' (Jer. 23:10–15, emphasis added)

Then they will cry out to the LORD, but he will not answer them. At that time he will hide his face from them because of the evil they have done.... 'As for the prophets who lead my people astray, they proclaim 'peace' if they have something to eat, but prepare to wage war against anyone who refuses to feed them. Therefore night will come over you, without visions, and darkness, without divination. The sun will set for the prophets, and the day will go dark for them. The seers will be ashamed and the diviners disgraced. They will all cover their faces because there is no answer from God.' (Micah 3:4–7)

As mercy's sweet voice died away, fear and horror seized the wicked.... Those who had not prized God's Word were hurrying to and fro, wandering from sea to sea, and from the north to the east, to seek the Word of the Lord.... What would they not give for one word of approval from God! (*Early Writings*, p. 281)

To the law and to the testimony: If they speak not according to this word, it is because there is no light in them. Distressed and hungry, they will roam through the land; when they are famished, they will become enraged and, looking upward, will curse their king and their God. Then they will look toward the earth and see only distress and darkness and fearful gloom, and they will be thrust into utter darkness. (Isa. 8:20, KJV; verses 21, 22, NIV)

I believe the fourth trumpet to be the time when papal leadership will become more prominent around the world, with Sunday worship becoming more of an issue. This is intimated in the trumpet lineup because only those who have the seal of God in their foreheads are protected from the terrible suffering described during the fifth trumpet, which is called the first of three woes. Thus the spiritual darkness of the fourth trumpet, followed by the sealed and protected people in the fifth trumpet, indicates that the Sunday law has no doubt taken place somewhere in this time period.

In Chapter 1 of this book, we considered the four stages of the removal of the Holy Spirit from the earthly temple, as described in Ezekiel 10 and 11. In order to set the stage for deeper insights into the fourth trumpet, I now want to go back to the book of Ezekiel. In chapters 8 and 9, there are four distinct stages outlined in the spiritual decline of Israel that caused God to remove His presence from the earthly sanctuary.

Notice the pattern of "four" reflected here. The progression of the four evils listed below from Ezekiel 8 and 9 precipitate the four stages of the withdrawal of the Holy Spirit in chapters 10 and 11. It is also interesting to note that in the historic view of the trumpets, the first four trumpets brought about the fall of Rome, which was then followed by war with Islam in the fifth and sixth trumpets (see chapter 4 of this book). In the study of the modern trumpets considered in this book, there are four stages that take America down, followed by war with Islam on a worldwide scale (see chapter 2 of this book).

Here is the list of the four progressive evils according to Ezekiel 8:

#1. The idol of jealously stood in the inner court (verse 3).
#2. Priests were officiating before the golden altar in the Holy Place, but they were secretly worshipping the idols of their own imaginations, which were portrayed all over the walls (verses 10–12).
#3. Women lead out in false worship (verse 14).
#4. Sun worship practiced (verse 16).

If we apply this list to our modern day spiritual illnesses, we can readily see that the first could apply to worldliness in the church, the second to the impact of the media on all levels of society, and thirdly, inappropriate leadership of women in the church. Please notice that I am not saying that women should have no roles of service in the church. Far from it! God calls for godly women to serve in all the ways in which God has gifted and called them. But for every truth, Satan has a counterfeit. Notice an example of this in Isaiah 3:12–14: "Youths oppress my people, women rule over them. My people, your guides lead you astray; they turn you from the path. The LORD takes his place in court; he rises to judge the people. The LORD enters into judgment against the elders and leaders of his people." (Please read the rest of the chapter. Contrast it with God's women, who are described in chapter 4 of Isaiah.)

Why does God judge the elders and leaders of His people? I believe it is because they are permitting the influence of the worldly women and unconsecrated youths to bring in the unholy music and fashions of the world into the church. Notice this statement by Ellen G. White:

> Isaiah 3, was presented before me. I was shown that this prophecy has its application to these last days; and the reproofs are given to the daughters of Zion who have thought only of appearance and display. Read verse 25: *'Thy men shall fall by the sword, and thy mighty in the war.'* I was shown that this scripture will be strictly fulfilled.... They will be brought low in the dust, and long for an experience in the things of God, which they failed to obtain. (*Spiritual Gifts*, vol. 4b, p. 63, emphasis added)

Is it possible that in our time this could be fulfilled in the war with Islam that is predicted in the fifth and sixth trumpets? Time will tell as the scroll of prophecy continues to unroll. Now, let's go back to the fourth step mentioned in Ezekiel 8:15, 16:

> He said to me, 'Do you see this, son of man? You will see things that are even more detestable than this.' He then brought me into the inner court of the house of the LORD, and there at the entrance to the temple ... were about twenty-five men. *With their backs toward the temple of the LORD and their faces toward the east, they were bowing down to the sun in the east.* (emphasis added)

I believe the fourth and final step that causes the withdrawal of the Holy Spirit is the passing of the national Sunday law. If we follow the chronology of the results of sun worship as described in Ezekiel 8, we see the man clothed in linen in Ezekiel 9 placing a mark on the foreheads of God's true followers, which protects them from the slaughter of those who do not receive the mark of God's approval.

> 'Go throughout the city of Jerusalem and put a mark on the foreheads of those who grieve and lament over all the detestable things that are done in it.' As I listened, he said to the others, 'Follow him through the city and kill, without showing pity or compassion. Slaughter the old men, the young men and women,

the mothers and children, *but do not touch anyone who has the mark.*' (Ezek. 9:4–6, emphasis added)

Notice the similarity of what occurs in the fifth trumpet.

And out of the smoke locusts came down on the earth and were given power like that of scorpions of the earth. They were told not to harm the grass of the earth or any plant or tree, *but only those people who did not have the seal of God on their foreheads.* (Rev. 9:3, 4, emphasis added)

The distinguishing mark in Revelation is 'the seal of God' and, like the mark in Ezekiel, is based on character qualifications. God places His mark of approval upon all who, through the power of the Holy Spirit, reflect the image of Jesus (see Ellen G. White, *Christ's Object Lessons*, p. 69). This stamp of approbation is God's mark of ownership, inscribed upon those who qualify for citizenship in His kingdom—(See Ellen G. White, *Testimonies to Ministers and Gospel Workers*, p. 446). The outward, visible sign of this completion of the work of grace in the soul will be the observance of the true Sabbath of the Bible (see *Testimonies for the Church*, vol. 8, p. 117).

Those who do not receive the mark will be those who are "satisfied with a mere desire to do right. But the Lord cannot change His standard. To do so would be to change Himself" (*The Seventh-Day Adventist Bible Commentary*, vol. 4. p. 607, emphasis added). Interestingly, the Hebrew word "mark" is really just the last letter of the alphabet, "*taw.*" It indicates "the end," or the finished product of God's work of grace. Similarly, the word used for "mark" in Revelation comes from the Greek word, "*charakter,*" meaning "exact representation, reproduction." NIV Concordance. Jesus is the "*aleph-taw,*" the "Alpha and Omega" (Rev. 1:8), the "Beginning and the End" (Rev. 21:6), the "Author and Finisher (KJV), or Perfecter (NIV) of our faith" (Heb. 12:2).

Thus, those who receive the seal of God, or mark in their foreheads, will fully represent Jesus in their characters. With them, Jesus has completed His work of redemption. Just as He rested on the seventh day after finishing His work of creation, so now He can come to claim His cleansed bride and take her home to live with Him forever.

On the contrary, those who are lost will be "those whose hereditary and cultivated tendencies to wrong are not purged from them. Their hearts are not cleansed from defilement. They were given an opportunity to do a work for God, but this work they did not choose to do, because they wished to carry out their own plans" (*The Seventh-day Adventist Bible Commentary*, vol. 4, p. 1160).

It is up to us to choose in which group we will be found when probation closes. That is why the messages God sends through the trumpets is so vital. They are calling us to prepare while there is still time.

> Just as soon as the people of God are sealed in their foreheads—it is not any seal or mark that can be seen, but a settling into the truth, both intellectually and spiritually, so they cannot be moved—just as soon as God's people are sealed and prepared for the shaking, it will come. *Indeed, it has begun already; the judgments of God are now upon the land, to give us warning, that we may know what is coming.* (*The Seventh-Day Adventist Bible Commentary*, vol. 4, p. 1161)

8 Hands Across the Gulf

And I saw a beast coming out of the sea. It had ten horns and seven heads, with ten crowns on its horns.... The dragon gave the beast his power and his throne and great authority. One of the heads of the beast seemed to have had a fatal wound, but the fatal wound had been healed. The whole world was filled with wonder and followed the beast. People worshiped the dragon because he had given authority to the beast, and they also worshiped the beast and asked, 'Who is like the beast? Who can wage war against it...?' And it was given authority over every tribe, people, language and nation. All inhabitants of the earth will worship the beast—all whose names have not been written in the Lamb's book of life, the Lamb who was slain from the creation of the world. Whoever has ears, let them hear. (Rev. 13:1–9)

Papal activity has been escalating since their rights to sovereignty over Vatican City and international affairs was restored by the Lateran Treaty in 1929 (see chapter 3 of this book). However, in recent years this growth in power has taken a definite upsurge, and with it a growing pressure to idealize Sunday observance as a necessity for all Christians, and indeed for all people. Here are some examples of this trend.

According to the papacy, Saturday is "no longer" the worship day of God—only on Sunday can we become part of the body of Christ in the world; only by worshiping on Sunday can we avoid "egoistic isolation" and instead be united "in a great community ... a universal community" becoming "related to everyone in the world" (*Address of His Holiness Benedict XVI*, July 25, 2005).

The papacy has also stated that "social disorder, war, injustice and violence" can only be countered "by renewed appreciation and respect for the universal moral law," meaning Sunday observance. Only by recognizing that law can the world have "dignity, life and freedom" with "conditions of justice and peace" in all the communities of the world. The promotion and defense of this law is what "must govern relations between nations and peoples in the pursuit of the common good of the human family ... within the international community" (*Address of His Holiness Benedict XVI to H.E. Mr. Francis Rooney New Ambassador of the United States of America to the Holy See*, November 12, 2005).

According to the Vatican, individuals cannot be sanctified except on Sunday. Christ transferred Sabbath sacredness to Sunday, and only those who keep Sunday belong to Christ. On November 27, 2006, Pope Benedict XVI wrote a letter to Cardinal Francis Arinze saying that only on Sunday does "the Risen Lord makes himself present among his followers", and only those who worship God on that day "worship God properly." His final wish is to soon see Sunday "regain all its importance."

Later, on February 22, 2007, Pope Benedict XVI gave an address in Rome stating that Sunday is an "obligation for all the faithful" that brings "authentic freedom enabling them to live each day." It is "the Lord's Day, a day to be sanctified," and those who do not keep it suffer "the loss of an authentic sense of Christian freedom" and the loss of being "the children of God." Sunday is the "primordial holy day" and "is meant to be kept holy," "a day of rest from work," which hopefully "will also be recognized by civil society" by law.

Several months later, on September 9, 2007, he declared, "Without the Lord's day, we cannot live," in Vienna, Austria. He continued saying that meeting with the Lord only occurs on the "specific day" of Sunday. Life does not flourish without Sunday; it is a day of rest, of freedom and equality for the whole world.

Speaking to the new Ambassador of the United States to the Holy See, Mary Ann Glendon, on February 29, 2008, Pope Benedict XVI encouraged America to exercise "its leadership within the international community" based on "the common moral law," referring to Sunday holiness. After the fall of the economy in September 2008, Pope Benedict XVI, in his encyclical, *Charity in Truth*, called for the creation of "a true world political authority." He stated that "such an authority would need to be universally recognized and to be vested with the effective power to ensure security.... It would have to have the authority to ensure compliance with its decisions."

It is my personal belief that the actual time of spiritual darkness predicted in the fourth trumpet began as a result of the bold public stand taken by the pope at the Seventh World Meeting of Families, held in Milan, Italy, from May 30 to June 3, 2012. Here is a quote taken directly from Pope Benedict XVI's homily on Sunday, June 3, 2012:

One final point: man, as the image of God, is also called to rest and to celebrate. The account of creation concludes with these words: 'And on the seventh day God finished his work which he had done, and he rested on the seventh day from all his work which he had done. So God blessed the seventh day and hallowed it' (Gen. 2:2–3). For us Christians, the feast day is Sunday, the Lord's day, the weekly Easter. It is the day of the Church, the assembly convened by the Lord around the table of the word and of the eucharistic Sacrifice, just as we are doing today, in order to feed on him, to enter into his love and to live by his love. It is the day of man and his values: conviviality, friendship, solidarity, culture, closeness to nature, play, sport. It is the day of the family, on which to experience together a sense of celebration, encounter, sharing, not least through taking part in Mass. Dear families, despite the relentless rhythms of the modern world, do not lose a sense of the Lord's Day! It is like an oasis in which to pause, so as to taste the joy of encounter and to quench our thirst for God.

What a bold challenge the pope's statements threw in the face of God's holy law, and of His Sabbath, the crowning act of His creation! How true and appropriate were the words of the pope in identifying that Sunday "is the day of man and his values," even including "play" and "sport." No wonder the number of the beast is 666 (Rev. 13:18). God says, "Six days shalt thou labour and do all thy work: But the seventh day is the sabbath of the LORD thy God: in it thou shalt not do any work" (Exod. 20:9, 10, KJV).

Six is the number of humankind's allotted days to work, which includes Sunday, the first day of the week. Playing sports or attending sports events is also a part of our values and works. But on the seventh day of Creation week, God rested from *all* His work and spent the day communing and fellowshipping with Adam and Eve, whom He had just created for that purpose. Since the fall of humanity, the Sabbath is also a symbol and weekly reminder that we must not trust in our own efforts to obtain salvation by our works. Instead, we are to trust wholly in the merits of our Savior and in His power to live out His righteous life in us. That is why the Sabbath is the sign or seal of God's approval of His people just before His second coming (see Rev. 7:3, 4), for they also will have ceased from all their works and will be in perfect harmony with His will in every area of their minds (see 2 Cor. 1:21, 22; Eph. 1:13, 14).

'Do not work for food that spoils, but for food that endures to eternal life, which the Son of Man will give you. For on him God the Father has placed his seal of approval.' Then they asked him, 'What must we do to do the works God requires?' Jesus answered, 'The work of God is this: to believe in the one he has sent.' (John 6:27–29)

God's law reaches the feelings and motives, as well as the outward acts. (*The Seventh-day Adventist Bible Commentary*, vol. 5, p. 1085)

If man is to become immortal, his mind must be in harmony with God's mind. (*Testimonies on Sexual Behavior, Adultery, and Divorce*, p. 116)

Holiness is agreement with God. (*Testimonies for the Church*, vol. 5, p. 743)

There remains, then, a Sabbath-rest for the people of God; for anyone who enters God's rest also rests from their works, just as God did from his. (Heb. 4:9, 10)

This calls for wisdom. Let the person who has insight calculate the number of the beast, for it is the number of man. That number is 666. (Rev. 13:18)

At this time I want to turn to present events that point to the deepening spiritual darkness of the fourth trumpet. In 2013, Pope Benedict XVI resigned, and Pope Francis was elected. Since then, the new pope seems to have taken the world by storm. "In a very short time, a vast, global, ecumenical audience has shown a hunger to follow him" ("Pope Francis, The Choice," *TIME*, December 11, 2013). He has also been called a "Jesuit's Jesuit" (Catholic News Service, http://www.catholicnews.com/, [accessed September 26, 2015]). Here is a comment on the Jesuit order taken from *The Great Controversy*:

> Vowed to perpetual poverty and humility, it was their studied aim ... to be devoted to the overthrow of Protestantism, and the re-establishment of the papal supremacy. When appearing as members of their order, they wore a garb of sanctity, visiting prisons and hospitals, ministering to the sick and the poor,

professing to have renounced the world, and bearing the sacred name of Jesus, who went about doing good. But under this blameless exterior the most criminal and deadly purposes were often concealed. It was a fundamental principle of the order that the end justifies the means.... The Jesuits rapidly spread themselves over Europe, and wherever they went, there followed a revival of popery. (pp. 234, 235)

Since taking office Pope Francis has certainly ingratiated himself into the hearts of millions of people around the globe. True to his calling, he has openly served the poor on the streets and other places until he has become known as the pope of the poor. President Obama has regularly spoken of his admiration for Francis, repeatedly praising the pontiff for his compassion and modesty.

Pope Francis has also taken an active leadership role around the world, visiting many countries and meeting with heads of state. "Francis is widely credited with helping to kickstart the secret diplomacy between Cuba and the United States.... According to a Vatican statement, Francis wrote letters to US and Cuban leaders ... in order to initiate a new phase in relations between the two parties" (Associated Newspapers Ltd., http://www.dailymail.co.uk/, [accessed September 26, 2015]).

Perhaps Pope Francis' greatest contribution to ecumenicalism is the historic live seven-minute video communication with Bishop Tony Palmer, which "was played before a gathering of Pentecostal preachers at the Kenneth Copeland Ministries annual ministers conference, held January 21, 2014, in Fort Worth, Texas.... Palmer called for unity between Protestants and Catholics. 'Brothers and sisters,' Palmer declared, 'Luther's protest is over. Is yours?'" ("Speaking as a Brother," *Liberty*, November/December, 2014).

By this action, a prophecy written more than 125 years ago is in the process of fulfillment:

> Through the two great errors, the immortality of the soul and Sunday sacredness, Satan will bring the people under his deceptions. While the former lays the foundation of spiritualism, the latter creates a bond of sympathy with Rome. The Protestants of the United States will be foremost in stretching their hands across the gulf to grasp the hand of spiritualism; they will reach over the abyss to clasp hands with the Roman power; and under the influence of this threefold union, this country will follow in

the steps of Rome in trampling on the rights of conscience. (*The Great Controversy*, p. 588)

On June 25, 2014, in the homily given at St. Peter's Square, Pope Francis stated:

> We are not isolated and we are not Christians on an individual basis, each one on his or her own, no, our Christian identity is to belong! We are Christians because we belong to the Church. It is like a last name: if the first name is 'I am a Christian,' the last name is 'I belong to the Church....' "No one becomes Christian by him- or herself. Christians are not made in a laboratory.... No one becomes Christian on his or her own.... In the Church there is no 'do it yourself,' there are no 'free agents....' At times one hears someone say: 'I believe in God, I believe in Jesus, but I don't care about the Church....' And this is not good. There are those who believe they can maintain a personal, direct and immediate relationship with Jesus Christ outside the communion and the mediation of the Church. These are dangerous and harmful temptations.

On June 18, 2015, Pope Francis released an encyclical on possible solutions for climate change. This was a particularly important encyclical for a couple of reasons:

> On June 18, 2015, Pope Francis' 183-page encyclical addressing climate change was released worldwide. Its title, 'Praised Be You,' is based on St. Francis of Assisi's ancient poetic 'Canticle of the Sun.' After bemoaning 'the breakdown of society' because of humanity's misguided materialism, secularism, and environmental negligence, Pope Francis seeks to bring 'the whole human family together' and help save the planet through a resurrection of spirituality and returning to God....Nestled firmly within this 183-page encyclical is a definite appeal from Pope Francis to the entire world to find 'a new start' by keeping Sunday as a day of rest. 'Sunday, like the Jewish Sabbath, is meant to be a day which heals our relationship with God, with ourselves, with others, and with the world' penned the Pope. 'In this way, Christian spirituality incorporates the value of relaxation and festivity.' (White Horse Media, https://www.whitehorsemedia.com, [accessed September 26, 2015]).

> The Pope's new 'climate change' encyclical ... includes a strong appeal to all nations to KEEP SUNDAY as part of a global solution to Planet Earth's escalating environmental crisis. Significantly, the same day that the Pope's encyclical was released, President Obama heartily affirmed 'His Holiness Pope Francis's encyclical,' even stating that 'the United States must be a leader in this effort' to help save the planet. (White Horse Media, https://www.whitehorsemedia.com, [accessed September 26, 2015]).

Doesn't this sound like the fulfillment of Revelation 13:11, 12 has begun to take place?

> Then I saw another beast, coming out of the earth. It had two horns like a lamb, but it spoke like a dragon. It exercised all the authority of the first beast on his behalf, and made the earth and its inhabitants worship the first beast, whose fatal wound had been healed.

Prophecy is rapidly fulfilling before our eyes, and we must be awake to what is happening while there is still time to prepare and sound the trumpet for others who may not know the meaning of these things.

What is yet to come? At the writing of this book, the Pope is scheduled to arrive in the United States on September 22, 2015. While here, he will visit the White House, speak to our Congress, and address the United Nations. This is the first time a pope has spoken to our Congress; who can predict what he will say? We cannot ignore the fact that this is a part of the fulfillment of end-time prophecy. What is our duty at this momentous time in history?

> The Lord in compassion is seeking to enlighten the understanding of those who are now groping in the darkness of error. He is delaying His judgments upon an impenitent world, in order that His light bearers may seek and save that which is lost. He is now calling upon His church on the earth to awake from the lethargy that Satan has sought to bring upon them, and fulfill their heaven-appointed work of enlightening the world. (*Testimonies to Ministers and Gospel Workers*, p. 458)

> Arise, shine, for your light has come, and the glory of the LORD rises upon you. See, darkness covers the earth and thick darkness

is over the peoples, but the LORD rises upon you and his glory appears over you. Nations will come to your light, and kings to the brightness of your dawn. (Isa. 60:1–3)

9 Knowing the Time

As he [Jesus] approached Jerusalem and saw the city, he wept over it and said, 'If you, even you, had only known on this day what would bring you peace—but now it is hidden from your eyes. The days will come upon you when your enemies will build an embankment against you and encircle you and hem you in on every side. They will dash you to the ground, you and the children within your walls. They will not leave one stone on another, because you did not recognize the time of God's coming to you.' (Luke 19:41–44)

Knowing the time—how important it is to know when prophecy is being fulfilled! How can we avoid sleeping through the alarm clock of current events that are telling us that our time of preparation is running out? It is absolutely vital to us and to our children to read the signs correctly—to hear and heed the trumpets sounding for our time!

God has always given men warning of coming judgments. Those who had faith in His message for their time, and who acted out their faith, in obedience to His commandments, escaped the judgments that fell upon the disobedient and unbelieving. (*The Desire of Ages*, p. 634)

For His church in every generation God has a special truth and a special work.... In every age there is a new development of truth, a message of God to the people of that generation. (*Christ's Object Lessons*, p. 78, 127)

When the time comes for a prophecy to be fulfilled, there is always the danger that the majority of people will have become complacent with the light they already have and see the continued development of light as something dangerous. This is what happened in Jesus' day.

> I was pointed back to the proclamation of the first advent of Christ. John was sent in the spirit and power of Elijah to prepare the way of Jesus. Those who rejected the testimony of John were not benefitted by the teachings of Jesus. Their opposition to the message that foretold His coming placed them where they could not readily receive the strongest evidence that He was the Messiah.... In doing this they placed themselves where they could not receive the blessing on the day of Pentecost, which would have taught them the way into the heavenly sanctuary. (*Early Writings*, p. 259)

> As we take up the study of God's word, we should do so with humble hearts. All selfishness, all love of originality, should be laid aside. Long-cherished opinions must not be regarded as infallible. It was the unwillingness of the Jews to give up their long-established traditions that proved their ruin. They were determined not to see any flaw in their own opinions or in their expositions of the Scriptures; but however long men may have entertained certain views, if they are not clearly sustained by the written word, they should be discarded. (*Counsels to Writers and Editors*, p. 36, 37)

> There is no excuse for anyone in taking the position that there is no more truth to be revealed, and that all our expositions of Scripture are without an error. The fact that certain doctrines have been held as truth for many years by our people, is not a proof that our ideas are infallible. Age will not make error into truth, and truth can afford to be fair. No true doctrine will lose anything by close investigation. (*Counsels to Writers and Editors*, p. 35)

> Whenever the people of God are growing in grace, they will be constantly obtaining a clearer understanding of His word. They will discern new light and beauty in its sacred truths. This has been true in the history of the church in all ages, and thus it will continue to the end. But as real spiritual life declines, it has ever been the tendency to cease to advance in the knowledge of the truth. Men rest satisfied with the light already received

from God's word, and discourage any further investigation of the Scriptures. They become conservative, and seek to avoid discussion. (*Counsels to Writers and Editors*, p. 38)

The purpose of this book is to bring out a further understanding of the meaning and application of the seven trumpets of Revelation than could have been seen even a generation ago because the events that we are now seeing were still in the future. Remember that Jesus said, "I am telling you now before it happens, so that when it does happen you will believe" (John 13:19). "I have told you this, so that when their time comes you will remember that I warned you" (John 16:4). Prophecies are to be recognized when they actually occur. When Daniel was given visions that he did not understand, he was told:

I am going to tell you what will happen later in the time of wrath, because the vision concerns the appointed time of the end. (Dan. 8:19)

Go your way, Daniel, because the words are rolled up and sealed until the time of the end. Many will be purified, made spotless and refined, but the wicked will continue to be wicked. None of the wicked will understand, but those who are wise will understand. (Dan. 12:9, 10)

It is interesting to note that even when the prophecy is unveiled, only the wise will understand. True wisdom comes only to those who are studying the prophecies with a heart open to the Holy Spirit's revealing. Human wisdom cannot ever understand the mysteries of God; trusting in your own wisdom will never be enough.

Those who are wise will shine like the brightness of the heavens, and those who lead many to righteousness, like the stars for ever and ever. But you, Daniel, roll up and seal the words of the scroll until the time of the end. (Dan. 12:3, 4)

Those are exciting words because that is exactly where we are now. We are standing on the verge of eternity, and it is time for us to open our eyes and pray that we will be among the wise who understand the meaning of the signs of *our* times!

At this point, I want to bring out different Biblical signs that are familiar throughout Scripture. They throw light on the seven trumpets as warnings for the final generation that the end is near. The first phenomenon that I want to point out is that each of the first four trumpets has been approximately three and a half years apart. No one could have known this before they occurred, yet as we look back now, this is quite clear. For clarity, I will give the outline to you:

> #1. The fall of the towers—September 11, 2001
> #2. Natural disasters—Two tsunamis, occurring on Christmas, 2004, and Easter, 2005, followed by hurricanes Katrina and Rita, plus many other disasters around the globe
> #3. Fall of the economy—September, 2008
> #4. Escalation of papal power and popularity—May/June 2012

The very fact that there is a regularity of time between the trumpets tells us that these are not just random accidental happenings on planet Earth. The timing means that there is a Divine Designer with a message. What is God trying to say by this purposeful planning of events?

Before we look at some verses to answer this question, it is important to recognize that the Bible is full of the significance of the number seven, or divisions or multiples of seven. There are far too many of these to consider them all here. But there are significant ones such as the seven days of creation, the seventh-day Sabbath, the seven steps in the sanctuary service, and the many "sevens" in the rituals of the sanctuary, such as the cleansing and dedication of the priests, etc. The number seems to stem from the fact that there are seven aspects of the Holy Spirit, which is symbolized in the sanctuary by the seven-branched candlestick, found in the Holy Place.

> After this I looked, and there before me was a door standing open in heaven. And the voice I had first heard speaking to me like a trumpet said, 'Come up here, and I will show you what must take place after this.' At once I was in the Spirit, and there before me was a throne in heaven with someone sitting on it.... From the throne came flashes of lightning, rumblings and peals of thunder. In front of the throne, seven lamps were blazing. These are the seven spirits of God. (Rev. 4:1, 2, 5)
>
> Then I saw a Lamb, looking as if it had been slain, standing at the center of the throne, encircled by the four living creatures

and the elders. The Lamb had seven horns and seven eyes, which are the seven spirits of God sent out into all the earth. (Rev. 5:6)

In this throne room scene, we see the whole Godhead—Father, Son, and Holy Spirit—working together for the salvation of humankind. The seven spirits are depicted as being in two places—one directly before the throne, and the second as being used by Jesus as the agent through which He will reach every person on Earth with the offer of His salvation. These seven spirits are delineated for us in Isaiah:

> A shoot will come up from the stump of Jesse; from his roots a Branch will bear fruit. The Spirit of the LORD will rest on him—the Spirit of *wisdom*, and of *understanding*, the Spirit of *counsel* and of *might*, the Spirit of *knowledge* and of the *fear of the LORD*—and he will delight in the fear of the LORD.... With righteousness he will judge the needy, with justice he will give decisions for the poor of the earth. (Isa. 11:1–4, emphasis added)

> The Lord will ... cleanse the bloodstains from Jerusalem *by a spirit of judgment* and a spirit of fire. (Isa. 4:4, emphasis added)

> To fear the LORD is to hate evil. (Prov. 8:13)

In this Old Testament Messianic prophecy, we see the perfection of the character of Jesus spelled out for us in the seven aspects of the Holy Spirit, which is, of course, the character and power of God the Father as well. It seems to me that the number seven has to do with completion, or perfection, or the number that is necessary to be finished with something. For example: God finished creating the world in seven days. Noah was given seven of every kind of clean animal, and he was in the ark for seven days before the rain came. Jacob served Laban seven years each for his two wives. Just look in a Bible concordance, and you'll see that the list of "sevens" is quite extensive! There is certainly a lot to learn about the significance of the number "seven" in the Bible.

The most fascinating study of sevens is when we begin to see how God uses them in prophetic time lines. Notice this in Daniel 9:24:

> Seventy 'sevens' are decreed for your people and your holy city to finish transgression, to put an end to sin, to atone for wickedness, to bring in everlasting righteousness, to seal up vision and prophecy and to anoint the Most Holy Place.

Without going into a Bible study of this text, we can see that God's people were given a probationary time in which God's Spirit would witness to His people. This was first accomplished by His prophets and through His sanctuary and eventually through His own Son and the work of His followers. After this, the end of their probationary time as the chosen nation would close and pass to the Gentiles. The fulfillment of this prophecy was concluded in AD 34 when the Jewish leaders rejected the preaching of Stephen and stoned him to death (Acts 7:51–60). Saul, who at that scene witnessed and assisted in the stoning of Stephen, was later to become Paul, the apostle chosen to take the message of Jesus to the Gentiles. "The Lord said to Ananias, 'Go! This man is my chosen instrument to proclaim my name to the Gentiles and their kings and to the people of Israel" (Acts 9:15).

In AD 34, as had been predicted, the time of Jewish probation as a nation came to an end, and the baton passed to the Gentiles. What would the Gentiles do with the Gospel and the eternal truths passed on from creation? Only time would tell. Jesus spoke of this in a prophecy found in Luke 21:24–36, which has great importance for us today. This prophecy reads like the morning newspaper!

> *Jerusalem will be trampled on by the Gentiles until the times of the Gentiles are fulfilled.* There will be signs in the sun, moon and stars. On the earth, nations will be in anguish and perplexity at the roaring and tossing of the sea. People will faint from terror, apprehensive of what is coming on the world, for the heavenly bodies will be shaken. At that time they will see the Son of Man coming in a cloud with power and great glory. When these things begin to take place, stand up and lift up your heads, because your redemption is drawing near.... *Truly I tell you, this generation will certainly not pass away until all these things have happened....* Be careful, or your hearts will be weighed down with carousing, drunkenness and the anxieties of life, and that day will close on you suddenly like a trap. For it will come on all those who live on the face of the whole earth. Be always on the watch, and pray that you may be able to escape all that is about to happen, and that you may be able to stand before the Son of Man. (emphasis added)

> Christ presented before them [the disciples] an outline of the prominent events to take place before the close of time.... The prophecy which He uttered was twofold in its meaning; while foreshadowing the destruction of Jerusalem, it prefigured also

the terrors of the last great day.... Unmistakable signs would precede the awful climax. (*The Great Controversy*, p. 25)

It seems clear that the probationary time for the Gentiles (meaning the whole world because all races of people are now equal before God [Gal. 3:28, 29]) ends at the coming of Christ, and that there will be distinct, obvious, and worldwide signs that will show that their probation is coming to an end. Isn't it interesting that these are the exact, same signs that we are seeing today? Some think that the coming of Jesus will be as a thief in the night, and that will definitely be true of all who do not watch and interpret the warning signs properly. Remember in our first chapter we read that it was a matter of life and death that the Israelites understood and obeyed the meaning of the sounding of the trumpets. Let's read the quotation again to refresh our memory:

> The Levites were designated by the Lord as the tribe in the midst of whom the sacred ark was to be borne, Moses and Aaron marching just in front of the ark, and the sons of Aaron following near them, each bearing trumpets. They were to receive directions from Moses, which they were to signify to the people by speaking through the trumpets. These trumpets gave special sounds which the people understood, and directed their movements accordingly.... None who gave attention were left in ignorance of what they were to do. If any failed to comply with the requirements of the Lord ... they were punished with death.... For they would only prove themselves willingly ignorant.... If they did not know the will of God concerning them, it was their own fault. They had the same opportunities to obtain the knowledge imparted as others ... had, therefore their sin of not knowing, not understanding, was as great in the sight of God as if they had heard and then transgressed. (*Testimonies for the Church*, vol. 1, p. 651)

The same is true now. As Jesus said, "Be careful, or ... that day will close on you suddenly like a trap" (Luke 21:34). Can we see more clearly now how important it is for us to rightly interpret the *meaning* of the trumpets? Everyone on earth is seeing them, but how many are interpreting them appropriately? How many know that the trumpets are a countdown to Jesus' coming, even though it should be obvious, since the seventh and last trumpet is the trumpet of God, which will sound at His return! We are not looking for a specific time; we are looking for *a series of events* that lead up to His coming. We are to watch and listen for the sound of His trumpets!

> We are living in the most solemn period of this world's history. The destiny of earth's teeming multitudes is about to be decided.... We have not a moment to lose. *Events of vital importance are taking place around us*; we are on Satan's enchanted ground. Sleep not, sentinels of God; the foe is lurking near, ready at any moment, should you become lax and drowsy, to spring upon you and make you his prey. (*The Great Controversy*, p. 601, emphasis added)

Unfortunately, most of those who hear will not know how to interpret them rightly. Jesus addressed His generation with the same challenge. "Why is my language not clear to you? Because you are unable to hear what I say. You belong to your father, the devil.... Whoever belongs to God hears what God says. The reason you do not hear is that you do not belong to God" (John 8:43, 44, 47).

Most of the world today is under the spell of the evil one. The attractions of the world are more inviting to them than the humble pathway marked out for the followers of Jesus. Jesus said concerning the blindness of most who listened to Him: "Though seeing, they do not see; though hearing, they do not hear or understand.... Otherwise they might see with their eyes, hear with their ears, understand with their hearts and turn, and I would heal them" (Matt. 13:13, 15).

Dear friends, it is sad to think that although everyone on earth is seeing the rapidly-fulfilling events that will so soon bring human probation to a close, most professed Christians, and even many Seventh-day Adventists, are asleep on the verge of the kingdom. It is like children playing on the seashore, unaware that there is a tidal wave coming that will soon carry them all away. What more can God do to awaken us to our peril? Let us heed the admonition of Paul to the Romans:

> And that, knowing the time, that now it is high time to awake out of sleep: for now is our salvation nearer than when we believed. The night is far spent, the day is at hand: let us therefore cast off the works of darkness, and let us put on the armour of light.... But put ye on the Lord Jesus Christ, and make not provision for the flesh, to fulfil the lusts thereof. (Rom. 13:11–14, KJV)

Let us therefore follow after the things which make for peace, and things wherewith one may edify another. (Rom. 14:19, KJV)

10 The Appointed Time

For years I have wondered at the mystery of the special significance of the Biblical use of the "three" or "three and a half." It is used many times in Scripture and prophecy. We have already looked at the number seven and have seen how it is used to signify completion or perfection. But what special meaning does God have for a number that is only half of seven? An interesting passage of Scripture that may help us in our discovery is found in Hosea 6:1–3:

> Come, let us return to the LORD. He has torn us to pieces but he will heal us; he has injured us but he will bind up our wounds. After two days he will revive us; on the third day he will restore us, that we may live in his presence. Let us acknowledge the LORD; let us press on to acknowledge him. As surely as the sun rises, he will appear; he will come to us like the winter rains, like the spring rains that water the earth.

Here is described the spiritual journey of those who have backslidden from the Lord but recognize His invitation to come back and be restored into His favor once again. It is symbolized as a three-day spiritual journey, which is rewarded by the reception of the early and latter rains. I personally have experienced these three-day journeys over the course of my life and still wonder at the full significance and meaning of the cost of letting go of God even for a short period of time. Ellen White speaks about this in reference to Jesus' parents' experience when they lost sight of Him at the Temple when He was twelve years old.

> By one day's neglect they lost the Saviour; but it cost them three days of anxious search to find Him. So with us; by idle talk, evilspeaking, or neglect of prayer, we may in one day lose the Saviour's presence, and it may take many days of sorrowful

search to find Him, and regain the peace that we have lost.... When we become absorbed in worldly things so that we have no thought for Him ... we separate ourselves from Jesus and from the heavenly angels. These holy beings cannot remain where the Saviour's presence is not desired, and His absence is not marked. This is why discouragement so often exists among the professed followers of Christ.... If we are Christ's, our sweetest thoughts will be of Him. (*The Desire of Ages*, p. 83)

In capturing the importance and meaning of this three-day phenomenon, I believe we can learn something from a very important concept found in Scripture, which is centered in the phrase, "the appointed time." This is first used in Genesis 18:14, when the Divine Visitor informed Abraham that he and Sarah would have the promised heir "at the appointed time next year." An appointed time in Scripture, or *moed* in Hebrew, means a designated time for meeting an appointment that has previously been made. In the context of prophecy, *it is the time when the prophecy is to be fulfilled*.

The most well-known use of this word for Seventh-day Adventists is found in Daniel 8:19 and 11:35, concerning the appointed time for the cleansing of the heavenly sanctuary and of the time of the end. Paul also refers to the time of the judgment as being "the appointed time" (1 Cor. 4:5).

We can see how important it is for us to be aware of God's appointed times to meet with Him, whether it be the Sabbath, our daily worship times, or any time when God has an appointment with us personally or corporately at church. But the most important times of meeting with God is when a prophecy has a fulfillment in a certain generation. At those times, only those who are waiting, watching, and studying will be spiritually awake to recognize the time of their appointment.

I foretold the former things long ago, my mouth announced them and I made them known; then suddenly I acted, and they came to pass.... From the first announcement I have not spoken in secret; at the time it happens, I am there. (Isa. 48:3, 16)

That was certainly true when Abraham and Sarah were visited by the Lord to announce the time of the birth of Isaac. It was also true when Michael came to help Gabriel convince Cyrus to let God's people go back to the land of Israel at the end of the 70-year prophecy of Jeremiah 29:10. It was true when Jesus and His disciples came preaching that "the time is fulfilled" to His generation (Mark 1:15, KJV). And it was true of the precious Advent pioneers who preached the message of the judgment in 1844. All of these people received the promise with faith and joy and were enabled to share the message with their generation.

What a challenge to us who are seeing the signs that have been prophesied concerning the second coming of Jesus! We have the privilege of heralding the coming of the King! We must beware of becoming drowsy or unfaithful on the borders of the heavenly kingdom, for Jesus said, "When the Son of Man comes, will he find faith on the earth?" (Luke 18:8). He must have a people who will catch the vision and preach the good news to everyone. Jesus is coming again!

One of the most fascinating of prophetic numbers is that of the 1260 prophetic days or years, which is found five times in the books of Daniel and Revelation. These all refer to the duration of papal persecution during the Dark Ages, when the little horn was given power to persecute God's people (see Dan. 7:25; 12:7; Rev. 11:2, 3; 12:6, 14; 13:5). There has to be significance to the fact that so many things in Scripture happened during a period of three and a half years, or 1260 literal days. For example, Elijah's period of no rain was three and a half years. Paul was in the desert of Arabia for three years in preparation for his ministry (Gal. 1:18). Jesus' ministry was three and a half years. His disciples preached for three and a half years after His death, until the stoning of Stephen and the close of Jewish probation as a nation. It was three and a half years from the time the Roman armies first surrounded Jerusalem in the fall of AD 66, until they returned in the spring of AD 70 and destroyed the temple and the city.

What, if any, could be the meaning of this cyclical repetition of the three and a half days or years? From my observation, the common thread seems to be that it takes three and a half years to bring something to a completely finished state. Even the timing of the second coming of Jesus is governed by this principle, for Paul states that the man of sin (or lawlessness) must be revealed before Jesus can return.

> Don't let anyone deceive you in any way, for that day will not come until the rebellion occurs and the man of lawlessness is revealed, the man doomed to destruction. He will oppose and exalt himself over everything that is called God or is worshiped, so that he sets himself up in God's temple, proclaiming himself to be God.... And then the lawless one will be revealed, whom the Lord Jesus will overthrow with the breath of his mouth and destroy by the splendor of his coming. (2 Thess. 2:3, 4, 8)

Perhaps this helps us understand why God allowed His people to be given over to the papal power for 1260 years, until the court of heaven would sit and his power would be taken away forever (see Dan. 7:26). By this we can conclude that this is the time God allowed for Satan to display his purposes and the nature of his opposition to God's law, His government, and His people. By this process the true character of the "man of sin" will be revealed to the universe, judged by God and His saints, and prepared for destruction.

This is consistent with a very important principle in God's government—that of allowing freedom of choice. God gives ample opportunity for His created beings to choose whether they will love and serve Him with an intelligent appreciation of who He is and what He stands for while also understanding that all His ways are based upon love. In order to do this, He gives time and opportunity for everyone to see the validity of His requirements and the outworking of His principles versus the results of disobedience. This introduces the concept of the "harvest principle," which is apparent all throughout Scripture. This means that when the outworking of the purposes of God are complete, He acts.

> The Lord ... does not forget or neglect His children; but He permits the wicked to reveal their true character, that none who desire to do His will may be deceived concerning them. Again, the righteous are placed in the furnace of affliction, that they themselves may be purified ... and also that their consistent course may condemn the ungodly and unbelieving. God permits the wicked to prosper and to reveal their enmity against Him, that when they shall have filled up the measure of their iniquity all may see His justice and mercy in their utter destruction. (*The Great Controversy*, p. 48)

An example of this is shown when in mercy for the Canaanite nations God gave them 430 years of probationary time to accept or to reject His laws. He said to Abraham, "In the fourth generation your descendants will come back here, for the sin of the Amorites has not yet reached its full measure" (Gen. 15:16). And exactly 430 years later, to the very day (see Exod. 12:41), the Israelites left Egypt and headed for the Promised Land. The allotted time period of probation for the Canaanites was ended, and God's people accepted the challenge to move toward the fulfillment of His promises to them. As we considered in the previous chapter, this same principle is also displayed in His dealings with His own people, the Jewish nation. Thus, when Jesus came, His opening message to the world was, "The time is fulfilled, and the kingdom of God is at hand" (Mark 1:15, KJV).

It seems apparent that within God's set time periods are built in the aspects of His longsuffering and mercy, "not wanting anyone to perish, but everyone to come to repentance" (2 Peter 3:9). He gives time for repentance, but He also works to make sure that within the time allotted, all will have had their chance to see the issues and make a final decision. And "as soon as the grain is ripe, he puts the sickle to it, because the harvest has come" (Mark 4:29).

Now let's go back to our original premise that the number 1260 in days and/or years is specifically chosen as God's allotted time for allowing Satan to display the nature of his character, his intentions to take over God's government, and subvert His people and His truth. This was fulfilled during the Dark Ages of papal persecution.

What about the *short* time of papal resurgence after the deadly wound is healed? Will there be any parallel for God's people at the time of the end? Before answering this question, we need to look carefully at two very important key texts found in the Old Testament. These are the most notable ones that are used to show the validity of the year/day principle.

The first is found in Numbers 14:24. "*For forty years—one year for each of the forty days* you explored the land—you will suffer for your sins and know what it is like to have me against you" (emphasis added). This was fulfilled when the Israelites had to go back into the desert for forty years, and everyone more than twenty years of age, except Caleb and Joshua, died as a result of their unbelief and rebellion.

Notice now that the second text is exactly opposite: "After you have finished this, lie down again ... and bear the sin of the people of Judah. I have assigned you 40 days, a day for each year" (Ezek. 4:6). This text is *one day for every year* of Israel's sin, which God told Ezekiel to bear upon himself, although *he was not a participant in that sin*. This shows the *abbreviated time* needed for a righteous person to symbolically bear the results of the sins of those whom he or she is representing.

Thus, we see that when God is allowing human beings to work through the results of their own sins and come to an understanding of the nature of that sin and its consequences, it is a longer time period than when the results of a sin are being displayed and the punishment endured by one who is taking the place of the sinner, though not being personally guilty.

The major example of this principle is displayed in the life of Jesus. His fast of 40 days in the wilderness was commensurate with the 40 years of wandering for the children of Israel. Where they failed, He conquered Satan and was victorious. He then entered upon His ministry, and for three and a half years (1260 literal days). He endured every test that His people would have to endure during the 1260-year period of struggle with the powers of papal darkness. He went through this not only for them but also for all the faithful saints of God who throughout the ages of Earth's history have given and will yet give their lives in service for their Master.

Jesus was completely surrendered to His Father's will, and the plan of God was perfectly lived out in Him; therefore, the battle with the evil one could be "cut ... short in righteousness" (Rom. 9:28, KJV). Satan's character was completely displayed in that length of time. The universe needed to see no more to be convinced of the hatred and malignity of Satan, contrasted with the wonderful love and mercy of God, His justice in dealing with sin and sinners, and the necessity of the final destruction of the wicked at the end of time. That part of the plan of salvation was finished, and the death of Jesus sealed it for all time and eternity.

One thing remained to be accomplished before the redemption of humankind was complete. Jesus' purpose in coming here on such an expensive errand was to totally "destroy the works of the devil" (1 John 3:8, KJV). In order to do this, He must prove that what the Holy Spirit had accomplished in Him could also be accomplished in His people. His very name means that "he will save his people from their sins" (Matt. 1:21). To do this would necessitate revealing the works of the devil so clearly that every person would be able to make an intelligent choice. Because we are born in sin and the carnal nature is at enmity with God, it would take time to reveal all the facets of the rebellion of Lucifer to the satisfaction of everyone.

The long time period—the 1260 years, which God permitted to completely reveal the workings of the man of sin—therefore began. During that time pride, arrogance, doctrines of devils and every evil thing crept into the church. The darkness deepened as the centuries rolled by, until it seemed that the light of truth would be entirely extinguished. At last the display was complete, and Jesus moved into His final work in the heavenly Sanctuary—the investigative judgment. During this process all the atrocities and errors of the little horn power would be revealed and judged (see Dan. 7:26), in preparation for the eradication and blotting out of even the records of sin from the universe.

We are still in that judgment process. Since 1844, God's people have been sounding the three angels' messages of Revelation 14. The shaking and sealing of the Church has also been in process, but the sands in the hourglass are running low. The angels are loosening their hold upon the four winds of the earth. There is only a little space of time for the people of God to prepare for what is coming.

Rev. 13:11–15 prophesies a short time of resurgence, when the little horn power will once again be revealed, but with an even greater ability, and winsomeness to deceive. The universe will have one more chance to see what Satan will do when he is permitted to exercise his power over the people of this earth.

When Jesus comes again, there will be only two groups—those who have given themselves entirely to the evil one and those who follow Jesus through His final atonement work in the heavenly sanctuary and are pronounced "blameless" (Rev. 14:5). When these two groups are fully developed, Jesus will have completed the conditions that are necessary to give Him full legal rights to rescue His faithful ones and to destroy the wicked at His coming. But what are the conditions that Jesus must fulfill before His work is finished?

In Deuteronomy 19:15, we find this very important text: "One witness is not enough to convict anyone accused of any crime or offense they may have committed. A matter must be established by the testimony of two or three witnesses." If God should destroy sinners on the basis of the witness of the life of Christ alone, this question would ever remain: *Can God really eradicate the sin problem in the lives of fallen sinners who have been steeped in iniquity and captives of Satan?* Praise God, the mouths of all will be stopped when God produces His final remnant, who are cleansed and purified by the merits and sacrifice of His Son. They have learned to hate sin and to hunger and thirst after righteousness—and they are filled.

"The very image of God is to be reproduced in humanity. The honor of God, the honor of Christ, is involved in the perfection of the character of His people" (*The Desire of Ages*, p. 671). This final purified remnant is essential to the finishing of the work of Jesus in the heavenly sanctuary. In them, He has the second witness of the efficacy of His merits and His blood to remove and blot out all the sins of His people. These are a finished, living representation of the saved of all ages, who have fallen asleep in Jesus at various stages of their spiritual development. The final remnant is the "firstfruits" of the earth (Rev. 14:4), the example of what all true followers of Jesus would, or could, have been had they lived in our day and time with all the light that is shining upon this generation.

It is for this reason that the final remnant, like Ezekiel and Jesus who were representatives of their people but were not participants in their sins, can go through the three and a half years in literal time instead of prophetic, year-day time (see Rev. 10:6, 7). Of them it is said: "The remnant of Israel will not do iniquity" (Zeph. 3:13, KJV; see also Jer. 50:20).

At the same time, the little horn power who will persecute them will have reached the completion of development as the antichrist and representative of the character of Satan. They, too, will finish the work of transgression in literal time, for they need no more than that to display their true character (see 2 Thess. 2:5–12 and Rev. 17:8–11).

What a privilege we have to be the elect of God, the generation chosen to live at this time in history—the appointed time of the judgment and the culmination of all things. How can we complain of our hardships when we have such a privilege? Therefore, "let us throw off everything that hinders and the sin that so easily entangles," and, looking to Jesus, the Author and Finisher of our faith, "let us run with perseverance the race marked out for us" (Heb. 12:1, 2). Soon—much sooner than we may think—the battle will be over, and we will be at home with our Lord.

I have presented this study to show a Biblical perspective of the significance of the three and a half year periods, which we have observed in the frequency of the trumpet warning messages since 2001. I believe that this is God's way of showing that He is definitely involved, and true to form, each trumpet is being given the amount of time needed for the message to accomplish its purpose. Those who hear and respond will move into the circle of God's presence and protection. Those who do not will ignore or rebel, and they will move even farther away from responding to God's last merciful call to come into the ark of safety through a saving relationship with Jesus.

11 The Hiding Place

In the last days the mountain of the Lord's temple will be established as the highest of the mountains; it will be exalted above the hills, and all nations will stream to it. Many peoples will come and say, 'Come, let us go up to the mountain of the LORD, to the temple of the God of Jacob. He will teach us his ways, so that we may walk in his paths.' The law will go out from Zion, the word of the LORD from Jerusalem. (Isa. 2:2, 3)

If you recall I have stated earlier that the seven trumpets are God's last call to the people of earth to be protected from the seven last plagues, which will fall upon the impenitent. For review, here are the correlating quotations:

The seven angels stood before God to receive their commission. To them were given seven trumpets. The Lord was going forth to punish the inhabitants of the earth for their iniquity, and the earth was to disclose her blood and no more cover her slain. (*Manuscript Releases*, vol. 15, p. 219)

Go, my people, enter your rooms and shut the doors behind you; hide yourselves for a little while until his wrath has passed by. See, the LORD is coming out of his dwelling to punish the people of the earth for their sins. The earth will disclose the blood shed on it; the earth will conceal its slain no longer. (Isa. 26:20, 21) *Note: I believe the "rooms" spoken of here are referring to our prayer life and our personal relationship with God.*

When you pray, go into your room, close the door and pray to your Father, who is unseen. Then your Father, who sees what is done in secret, will reward you. (Matt. 6:6)

It is secret communion with God that sustains the soul-life. It was in the mount with God that Moses beheld the pattern of that wonderful building which was to be the abiding-place of His glory. It is in the mount with God—the secret place of communion—that we are to contemplate His glorious ideal for humanity. Thus we shall be enabled so to fashion our character-building that to us may be fulfilled the promise, 'I will dwell in them, and walk in them; and I will be their God, and they shall be My people.' (*Gospel Workers*, p. 254)

'Come now, let us settle the matter,' says the LORD. 'Though your sins are like scarlet, they shall be as white as snow; though they are red as crimson, they shall be like wool. If you are willing and obedient, you will eat the good things of the land; but if you resist and rebel, you will be devoured by the sword.' (Isa. 1:18–20)

Whoever dwells in the shelter of the Most High will rest in the shadow of the Almighty. I will say of the LORD, 'He is my refuge and my fortress, my God, in whom I trust.' Surely he will save you from the fowler's snare and from the deadly pestilence. He will cover you with his feathers, and under his wings you will find refuge; his faithfulness will be your shield and rampart. You will not fear the terror of night, nor the arrow that flies by day, nor the pestilence that stalks in the darkness, nor the plague that destroys at midday. A thousand may fall at your side, ten thousand at your right hand, but it will not come near you. You will only observe with your eyes and see the punishment of the wicked. If you say, 'The LORD is my refuge,' and you make the Most High your dwelling, no harm will overtake you, no disaster will come near your tent. For he will command his angels concerning you to guard you in all your ways. (Ps. 91:1–11)

It seems obvious that in this psalm David is referring to the Most Holy Place of the sanctuary, where the wings of the angels spread over the ark and cover the Shekinah Glory of God's presence and His holy law. Actually, the whole Bible is written in sanctuary language, and it is especially relevant to the final generation. It is important to realize that the final battles of Satan's war against God will revolve around the law of God, and especially the Sabbath.

God's commandment-keeping people stand under the broad shield of Omnipotence. (*Testimonies for the Church*, vol. 8, pp. 120, 121)

The Lord protects every human being who bears His sign. (*The Seventh-day Adventist Bible Commentary*, vol. 7, p. 969)

It is God that shields His creatures and hedges them in from the power of the destroyer. But the Christian world have shown contempt for the law of Jehovah; and the Lord will do just what He has declared He would—He will withdraw His blessings from the earth and remove His protecting care from those who are rebelling against His law.... Satan has control of all whom God does not especially guard. (*The Great Controversy*, p. 589)

What does the Old Testament sanctuary have to do with keeping God's people safe through the time of trouble and the seven last plagues? It is because there is a divinely inspired order in the sanctuary that enables our minds to comprehend spiritual things and to come into connection with the mind of God.

Son of man, describe the temple to the people of Israel, that they may be ashamed of their sins. Let them consider its perfection, and if they are ashamed of all they have done, make known to them the design of the temple—its arrangement, its exits and entrances—its whole design and all its regulations and laws. Write these down before them so that they may be faithful to its design and follow all its regulations. This is the law of the temple: All the surrounding area on top of the mountain will be most holy. Such is the law of the temple. (Ezek. 43:10–12)

We all need to keep the subject of the sanctuary in mind.... There is a sanctuary in heaven, and ... a pattern of this sanctuary was once built on this earth. God desires His people to become familiar with this pattern, keeping ever before their minds the heavenly sanctuary, where God is all and in all. (*The Seventh-day Adventist Bible Commentary*, vol. 7A, p. 482)

I saw that everything in heaven was in perfect order.... Said the angel, 'Behold ye and know how perfect, how beautiful the order in heaven; follow it.' (*Manuscript Releases*, vol. 5, p. 227)

The temple of God is opened in heaven, and the threshold is flushed with the glory which is for every church that will love God and keep His commandments. We need to study, to meditate, and to pray. Then we shall have spiritual eyesight to discern the inner courts of the celestial temple. (*Testimonies for the Church*, vol. 6, p. 368)

The vision given to Isaiah [Isa. 6:1–4] represents the condition of God's people in the last days. They are privileged to see by faith the work that is going forward in the heavenly sanctuary. (*The Seventh-day Adventist Bible Commentary*, vol. 4, p. 1139)

Seventh-day Adventists gained a deeper understanding and appreciation of the sanctuary after the disappointment in 1844, when it was revealed that Jesus had begun His closing work for humankind in His second-apartment ministry. In recent years it has become clearer to many that the whole sanctuary is a pattern for prayer and prepares us for the deeper work of cleansing that Jesus wants to do in our hearts. Briefly, these steps are:

#1. The Gate: "Enter his gates with thanksgiving and his courts with praise" (Ps. 100:4). We should praise God for all His goodness to us every day; we should live in the attitude of praise all day long.

#2. The Altar of Sacrifice: "If we confess our sins, he is faithful and just and will forgive us our sins and purify us from all unrighteousness" (1 John 1:9). We should confess our particular sins, weaknesses, and failings, as revealed to us by the Holy Spirit. We should ask for cleansing and victory day by day, moment by moment, and maintain an attitude of humility toward God and others.

#3. The Laver of Water: "Christ loved the church and gave himself up for her to make her holy, cleansing her by the washing with water through the word" (Eph. 5:25, 26). We should allow Jesus to cleanse us by applying the Word of God to our minds.

#4. The Seven-Branched Candlestick: "In front of the throne, seven lamps were blazing. These are the seven spirits of God" (Rev. 4:5). We should ask for the fruit of the Spirit: "love, joy, peace, forebearance, kindness, goodness, faithfulness, gentleness and self-control" (Gal. 5:22, 23).

#5. The Table of Shewbread: "I am the bread of life.... that comes down from heaven, which anyone may eat and not die" (John 6:48, 50). We should meditate upon Jesus' life and appropriate His example to our own experience. We should ask the Holy Spirit to impart and impute His righteousness into our lives.

#6. The Altar of Incense: "Another angel, who had a golden censer, came and stood at the altar. He was given much incense to offer, with the prayers of all God's people, on the golden altar in front of the throne" (Rev. 8:3). Our prayers should intercede for family, self, and others. We should keep our thoughts and prayers ascending to God throughout the day, even when we are busy with the duties of life.

#7. The Ark of the Covenant: "One thing I ask from the LORD, this only do I seek: that I may dwell in the house of the LORD all the days of my life, to gaze on the beauty of the LORD and to seek him in his temple. For in the day of trouble he will keep me safe in his dwelling; he will hide me in the shelter of his sacred tent and set me high upon a rock" (Ps. 27:4, 5). We should live in constant communion with God, surrender every thought, emotion and action to Him, and trust in Him completely on all matters.

Here is the antidote for all the darkness, sadness, and despair that the devil has heaped upon the human race from the beginning of sin. It is upbeat, positive, and healing to the mind and emotions. It gives hope and an outward focus. It lifts our minds from the circumstances in which we may find ourselves and places them upon God, our strength and eternal salvation. It places our minds in constant communion with the presence, power, and mind of God. It is the healing power of connection with God in His sanctuary.

> LORD, who may dwell in your sacred tent? Who may live on your holy mountain? The one whose walk is blameless, who does what is righteous, who speaks the truth from their heart; whose tongue utters no slander, who does no wrong to a neighbor, and casts no slur on others; who despises a vile person but honors those who fear the LORD; who keeps an oath even when it hurts, and does not change their mind; who lends money to the poor without interest; who does not accept a bribe against the innocent. Whoever does these things will never be shaken. (Ps. 15:1–5)

Now that we know what the hiding place is and how to enter it, let's review again the principles of the trumpets for the last generation. First, the trumpets are warnings of what is coming upon the earth as a result of the withdrawal of the Holy Spirit. Each trumpet is a sample of the impending and ultimate destruction of the whole earth as the actual presence of Jesus draws near to our planet.

Warning trumpets are tempered with God's grace calling out to the world to escape the results of the 6,000 years of sin and rebellion of the human race. The trumpets are God's voice giving the last call, saying to all who will understand and heed His message: "'Come out of her, my people,' so that you will not share in her sins, so that you will not receive any of her plagues; for her sins are piled up to heaven, and God has remembered her crimes" (Rev. 18:4, 5).

> After this I looked, and I saw in heaven the temple—that is, the tabernacle of the covenant law—and it was opened. Out of the temple came the seven angels with the seven plagues. They were dressed in clean, shining linen and wore golden sashes around their chests. Then one of the four living creatures gave to the seven angels seven golden bowls filled with the wrath of God, who lives for ever and ever. And the temple was filled with smoke from the glory of God and from his power, and no one could enter the temple until the seven plagues of the seven angels were completed. (Rev. 15:5–8)

The ministry of wrath unmingled with mercy then begins. In order to understand the seven last plagues, we first need to understand their connection with both the sanctuary and the trumpets. Both trumpets and plagues come out of the sanctuary and are a direct action from God to show the results of not heeding His truth. What a merciful God He has been to extend our probation to the extent that not one person will be left unwarned! Yet the last soul will be reached, the last decision made, and the door of mercy then closes forever for those who have refused to respond to His grace.

> When the third angel's message closes, mercy no longer pleads for the guilty inhabitants of the earth. The people of God have accomplished their work. They have received 'the latter rain,' 'the refreshing from the presence of the Lord,' and they are prepared for the trying hour before them. Angels are hastening to and fro in heaven. An angel returning from the earth announces that his work is done; the final test is brought upon the world, and all who have proved themselves loyal to the divine precepts have received 'the seal of the living God.' Then Jesus ceases His intercession in the sanctuary above. He lifts His hands and with a loud voice says, 'It is done.' (*The Great Controversy*, p. 613)

In 1991, I did a study comparing the steps in the sanctuary with the seven last plagues. Here I will give just a short synopsis to show that each plague is a result of not coming into the sanctuary, and thus having no protection from the burning wrath of God, which is poured out without mixture upon the earth after the close of human probation.

#1. Sores on the Body: "The first angel went and poured out his bowl on the land, and ugly, festering sores broke out on the people who had the mark of the beast and worshiped his image" (Rev. 16:2). This covers the sin of self-worship; there has been a lack of gratitude toward God and acknowledgment of His creatorship.

> The wrath of God is being revealed from heaven against all the godlessness and wickedness of people.... For although they knew God, they neither glorified him as God nor gave thanks to Him, but their thinking became futile and their foolish hearts were darkened.... Therefore God gave them over in the sinful desires of their hearts to sexual impurity for the degrading of their bodies with one another. They ... worshiped and served created things rather than the Creator—who is forever praised. Amen. Because of this, God gave them over to shameful lusts.... Men committed shameful acts with other men, and received in themselves the due penalty for their error. (Rom. 1:18–28)

#2. Sea Turned to Blood: "The second angel poured out his bowl on the sea, and it turned into blood like that of a dead person, and every living thing in the sea died" (Rev. 16:3). This speaks to the sin of rejecting the knowledge of God through Jesus. Many have refused to repent and be justified through the blood of Christ, spurning the wooing of God's love through the sacrifice of His Son, which is the only cure for hatred and cruelty in the human heart.

#3. Fountains and Rivers Turned to Blood: "The third angel poured out his bowl on the rivers and springs of water, and they became blood. Then I heard the angel in charge of the waters say: 'You are just in these judgments ... for they have shed the blood of your holy people and your prophets, and you have given them blood to drink as they deserve" (Rev. 16:4-6). This speaks to the sin of rejecting the cleansing, sanctifying work of Christ through the word of God and the Holy Spirit.

> Unless you eat the flesh of the Son of Man and drink his blood, you have no life in you. (John 6:53; see verses 54–63)

> On the last and greatest day of the festival, Jesus stood and said in a loud voice, 'Let anyone who is thirsty come to me and drink. Whoever believes in me, as Scripture has said, rivers of living

water will flow from within them.' *By this he meant the Spirit, whom those who believed in him were later to receive.* (John 7:37–39; emphasis added)

On that day a fountain will be opened to the house of David and the inhabitants of Jerusalem, to cleanse them from sin and impurity. (Zech. 13:1)

Because *I tried to cleanse you but you would not be cleansed* from your impurity, you will not be clean again until my wrath against you has subsided. (Ezek. 24:13, emphasis added)

#4. The Sun Scorches Men with Fire: "The fourth angel poured out his bowl on the sun, *and the sun was allowed to scorch people with fire.* They were seared by the intense heat and they cursed the name of God, who had control over these plagues, but *they refused to repent and glorify Him*" (Rev. 16:8, 9; emphasis added). This speaks of the sin of rejecting the light, guidance, purification, and transforming work of the Holy Spirit. This highlights those who will choose instead to follow the inclinations of the carnal heart.

He then brought me into the inner court of the house of the LORD, and there at the entrance to the temple, between the portico and the altar, were about twenty-five men. *With their backs toward the temple of the LORD and their faces toward the east, they were bowing down to the sun in the east.* (Ezek. 8:16; emphasis added)

'The Lord ... will come to his temple; the messenger of the covenant ... will come,' says the LORD Almighty. But who can endure the day of his coming? Who can stand when he appears? For he will be like a refiner's fire or launderer's soap.... He will purify the Levites and refine them. (Mal. 3:1–3, emphasis added)

The Lord will wash away the filth ... from Jerusalem by a *spirit of judgment and a spirit of fire.* (Isa. 4:4, emphasis added)

He will baptize you with the Holy Spirit and with fire. His winnowing fork is in his hand, and he will clear his threshing floor, gathering his wheat into the barn and *burning up the chaff with unquenchable fire.* (Matt. 3:11, 12, emphasis added)

> The bellows blow fiercely *to burn away the lead with fire, but the refining goes on in vain; the wicked are not purged out.* (Jer. 6:29, emphasis added)

> Surely the day is coming; it will burn like a furnace. All the arrogant and every evildoer will be stubble, and *that day that is coming will set them on fire,'* says the LORD Almighty. 'Not a root or a branch will be left to them.' (Mal. 4:1, emphasis added)

#5. Darkness on the Throne of the Beast: "The fifth angel poured out his bowl on the throne of the beast, and its kingdom was plunged into darkness. People gnawed their tongues in agony and cursed the God of heaven because of their pains and their sores, but they refused to repent of what they had done" (Rev. 16:10, emphasis added). This shows the sin of rejecting the authority and Lordship of Christ; it focuses on those choosing to follow the delusions of Satan and traditions of humankind and worshiping the beast and his image.

> When Jesus spoke again to the people, he said, 'I am the light of the world. Whoever follows me will never walk in darkness, but will have the light of life.' (John 8:12)

> Giving joyful thanks to the Father, who has qualified you to share in the inheritance of his holy people in the kingdom of light. For he has rescued us from the dominion of darkness and brought us into the kingdom of the Son he loves. (Col. 1:12, 13)

> That day will not come until the rebellion occurs and the man of lawlessness is revealed, the man doomed to destruction. *He will oppose and will exalt himself over everything that is called God or is worshiped, so that he sets himself up in God's temple, proclaiming himself to be God....* The lawless one will be revealed, whom the Lord Jesus will overthrow with the breath of his mouth and destroy by the splendor of his coming. (2 Thess. 2:3, 4; 8, emphasis added)

#6. Three Evil Spirits Working Miracles: *"The sixth angel poured out his bowl on the great river Euphrates, and its water was dried up to prepare the way for the kings from the East. Then I saw three impure spirits that looked like frogs; they came out of the mouth of the dragon, out of the mouth of the beast and out of the mouth of the false prophet. They are demonic spirits that perform* *signs,* and they go out to the kings of the whole world, to gather them for the battle on the great day of God Almighty.... Then they gathered the kings together to the place that in Hebrew is called Armageddon" (Rev. 16:12–14, 16; emphasis added).

This refers to the sin of choosing to listen to and believe the devil's deceptive lies. Some choose to communicate with evil spirits instead of with God and accept the devil's powers instead of appealing to God for His miraculous answer to the prayers of His saints.

> The Spirit clearly says that in later times some will abandon the faith and follow deceiving spirits and things taught by demons. (1 Tim. 4:1)

> Then I saw a second beast, coming out of the earth. It had two horns like a lamb, but it spoke like a *dragon. It exercised all the authority of the first beast on its behalf.... And it performed great signs,* even causing fire to come down from heaven to earth in full view of the people. Because of the signs it was given power to do on behalf of the first beast, *it deceived the inhabitants of the earth. It ordered them to set up an image in honor of the beast* ... and cause all who refused to worship the image to be killed. (Rev. 13:11–15; emphasis added)

> The coming of the lawless one will be in accordance with how Satan works. He will use all sorts of displays of power through *signs and wonders that serve the lie,* and all the ways that wickedness deceives those who are perishing. *They perish because they refused to love the truth and so be saved.* For this reason God sends them a powerful delusion so that they will believe the lie and so that all will be condemned who have not believed the truth but have delighted in wickedness. (2 Thess. 2:9–12, emphases added)

#7. The Voice of God Proclaims "It is Done;" the Nations Fall; A Severe Earthquake; Great Hailstones:

> The seventh angel poured out his bowl into the air, *and out of the temple came a loud voice from the throne, saying, 'It is done!'* Then there came flashes of lightning, rumblings, peals of thunder and a severe earthquake.... The great city [Babylon] split into three parts, and *the cities of the nations collapsed....* Every

island fled away and the mountains could not be found. From the sky *huge hailstones*, each weighing about a hundred pounds, fell upon men. And they cursed God on account of the plague of hail, because the plague was so terrible. (Rev. 16:17–21, emphasis added)

The seventh angel sounded his trumpet, and there were loud voices in heaven, which said: *'The kingdom of the world has become the kingdom of our Lord and of his Messiah, and He will reign for ever and ever....'* The time has come for judging the dead, and for rewarding your servants the prophets and your people who revere your name, both small and great—and for destroying those who destroy the earth. *Then God's temple in heaven was opened, and within his temple was seen the ark of his covenant.* (Rev. 11:15, 18, 19, emphasis added)

These texts acknowledge the sin of refusing to participate in the investigative judgment work of Christ by repentance and confession of sin.

Woe! Woe to you, great city.... In one hour she has been brought to ruin! Rejoice over her, you heavens! Rejoice, you people of God...! God has judged her with the judgment she imposed on you. (Rev. 18:19, 20)

After this I heard what sounded like the roar of a great multitude in heaven shouting: 'Hallelujah! Salvation and glory and power belong to our God, for *true and just are His judgments*. He has condemned the great prostitute who corrupted the earth by her adulteries. *He has avenged on her the blood of His servants....' Then a voice came from the throne, saying: 'Praise our God, all you His servants, you who fear Him, both great and small!'* (Rev. 19:1, 2, 5, emphasis added)

Then I saw a great white throne and him who was seated on it. The earth and the heavens fled from his presence, and there was no place for them. And I saw the dead, great and small, standing before the throne, and books were opened. Another book was opened, which is the book of life. *The dead were judged according to what they had done as recorded in the books....* Anyone whose name was not found written in the book of life was thrown into the lake of fire. (Rev. 20:11, 12, 15, emphasis added)

At that time Michael, the great prince who protects your people, will arise. There will be a time of distress such as has not happened from the beginning of nations until then. But *at that time your people—everyone whose name is found written in the book—will be delivered*. (Dan. 12:1, emphasis added)

How important it is that each of us heed the warning of the trumpets, come into the hiding place with Jesus, and bring our families and everyone who will listen and respond to the call of God. All who do this will be protected from the seven last plagues and be prepared to meet Jesus in peace at His coming.

12 Armageddon

The last three trumpets are called "woes."

As I watched, I heard an eagle that was flying in midair call out in a loud voice: 'Woe! Woe! Woe to the inhabitants of the earth, because of the trumpet blasts about to be sounded by the other three angels. (Rev. 8:13)

Throughout Scripture, woes are pronounced upon a generation whose probationary time is ending. An example is found in Luke 11:37–52. Christ pronounces six woes on the Pharisees, including the pronouncement in verses 50, 51: "Therefore this generation will be held responsible for the blood of all the prophets that has been shed since the beginning of the world.... Yes, I tell you, this generation will be held responsible for it all."

In Isaiah 5, there are recorded seven woes that were spoken to Israel, which sound very much like an end-time prophecy.

What more could have been done for my vineyard than I have done for it? When I looked for good grapes, why did it yield only bad? Now I will tell you what I am going to do to my vineyard: I will take away its hedge, and it will be destroyed; I will break down its wall, and it will be trampled.... For they have rejected the law of the LORD Almighty and spurned the word of the Holy One of Israel. Therefore the LORD's anger burns against his people; his hand is raised and he strikes them down. The mountains shake, and the dead bodies are like refuse in the streets. Yet for all this, his anger is not turned away, his hand is still upraised. He lifts up a banner for the distant nations, he whistles for those at the ends of the earth. Here they come, swiftly and speedily! Not one of them grows tired or stumbles, not one slumbers or sleeps.... Their arrows are sharp, all their bows are strung; their horses' hooves seem like flint, their chariot wheels like a whirlwind. Their roar is like that of a lion, they roar like young lions; they growl as they seize their prey and carry it off with no one to rescue. In that day they will roar over it like the roaring of the sea. And if one looks at the land, there is only darkness and distress; even the sun will be darkened by the clouds. (Isa. 5:4, 5, 24–30)

Notice how similar this sounds to the predictions of war that fall under the fifth and sixth trumpets.

The fifth angel sounded his trumpet, and I saw a star that had fallen from the sky to the earth. The star was given the key to the shaft of the Abyss. When he opened the Abyss, smoke rose from it like the smoke from a gigantic furnace. The sun and sky were darkened by the smoke from the Abyss. And out of the smoke locusts came down on the earth and were given power like that of scorpions of the earth. They were told not to harm the grass of the earth or any plant or tree, but only those people who did *not* have the seal of God on their foreheads. (Rev. 9:1–4, emphasis added)

Let's stop right here. According to volume seven of The Seventh-day Adventist Bible Commentary, it is generally thought that Satan is the fallen star and that the locusts represent the ravages of the Saracens and Turks, thus preparing the way for the Muslim conquest. But right in the middle of this passage is the telltale announcement that *these invading armies are not allowed to harm the people who have the seal of God on their foreheads* (see *The Seventh-day Adventist Bible Commentary*, vol. 7, p. 792). It is also interesting to note that in Ezekiel 9:4–6 the scene is similar:

'Go throughout the city of Jerusalem and put a mark on the foreheads of those who grieve and lament over all the detestable things that are done in it.... Slaughter the old men, the young men and women, the mothers and children, but *do not touch anyone who has the mark*. Begin at my sanctuary.' *So they began with the old men who were in front of the temple*. (emphasis added)

Please note that these elders were the ones who were worshipping the sun:

> He then brought me into the inner court of the house of the LORD, and there at the entrance to the temple ... were about twenty-five men. With their backs toward the temple of the LORD and their faces toward the east, they were bowing down to the sun in the east. (Ezek. 8:16)

Ellen White places this at the very end of time:

> The mark of deliverance has been set upon those 'that sigh and that cry for all the abominations that be done.' Now the angel of death goes forth, represented in Ezekiel's vision by the men with the slaughtering weapons.... *The work of destruction begins among those who have professed to be the spiritual guardians of the people. The false watchmen are the first to fall.* (*The Great Controversy*, p. 656, emphasis added)

What is it that makes sun worship so offensive to God? Let's go back to the Old Testament for more light on this issue. Baal and Ashtoreth were two leading heathen gods whom the Israelites loved to worship whenever they left the Lord (see Judges 2:10–22; 1 Kings 16:30–33). When Josiah became king of Israel, he destroyed Baal worship in Israel and reestablished the worship of Jehovah.

> The king ordered Hilkiah the high priest, the priests next in rank and the doorkeepers to remove from the temple of the LORD all the articles made for Baal and Asherah and all the starry hosts.... He did away with the idolatrous priests ... who burned incense to Baal, to the sun and moon, to the constellations and to all the starry hosts....He removed from the entrance to the temple of the LORD the horses that the kings of Judah had dedicated to the sun.... Josiah then burned the chariots dedicated to the sun. (2 Kings 23:4, 5, 11)

These gods were very offensive to God because their worship was licentious, and the sun, moon and stars were the objects of worship, in direct opposition to the first, second, and fourth commandments:

> You shall have no other gods before me. (Exod. 20:3)

You shall not make for yourself an image in the form of anything in heaven above or on the earth beneath or in the waters below. You shall not bow down to them or worship them. (Exod. 20:4, 5)

Remember the Sabbath day by keeping it holy. Six days you shall labor and do all your work, but the seventh day is a sabbath to the LORD your God.... For in six days the LORD made the heavens and the earth, the sea, and all that is in them, but he rested on the seventh day. Therefore the LORD blessed the Sabbath day and made it holy. (Exod. 20:8, 9, 11)

You see, the Sabbath issue is about God's creatorship. There can be no other gods besides Him because He has created everything that exists. The heavenly bodies are the work of His hands and are for service to all God's universe, creating heat, light, and beauty. Some are habitats for living creatures, as well as for many other aspects that are beyond our comprehension. When created beings worship created things, they are actually worshipping the very things that God has made to serve and bless us!

The wrath of God is being revealed from heaven against all the godlessness and wickedness of people ... since what may be known about God is plain to them.... For since the creation of the world God's invisible qualities—his eternal power and divine nature—have been clearly seen, being understood from what has been made, so that people are without excuse.... Although they claimed to be wise, they became fools and exchanged the glory of the immortal God for images made to look like a mortal human being and birds and animals and reptiles.... They exchanged the truth of God for a lie, and worshiped and served created things rather than the Creator. (Rom. 1:18–25)

A very important aspect of the fifth trumpet is that somewhere between the time of the fourth trumpet to the early stages of the fifth trumpet, the passing of the Sunday law, or at least the first stages of it, must have taken place in order for the seal of God to be placed upon their foreheads. This has a direct connection with Revelation 7:1–4:

After this I saw four angels standing at the four corners of the earth, holding back the four winds of the earth to prevent any wind from blowing on the land or on the sea or on any tree. Then I saw another angel coming up from the east, having the seal of the living God. He called out in a loud voice to the four angels who had been given power to harm the land and the sea: 'Do not harm the land or the sea or the trees until we put a seal on the foreheads of the servants of our God.' Then I heard the number of those who were sealed: 144,000 from all the tribes of Israel.

Here is pictured the people who are protected in the fifth seal—the 144,000. This group is highlighted again in Revelation 14:1–5:

Then I looked, and there before me was the Lamb, standing on Mount Zion, and with him 144,000 who had his name and his Father's name written on their foreheads.... These are those who did not defile themselves with women, for they remained virgins.... They were purchased from among mankind and offered as firstfruits to God and the Lamb. No lie was found in their mouths; they are blameless.

In the Bible a woman often symbolizes the church, or the bride of Christ. A pure woman represents the true people of God while an impure woman symbolizes a counterfeit or a mixture of truth and error. Here are some Scriptural examples:

A true church:
"I have likened the daughter of Zion to a comely and delicate woman" (Jer. 6:2, KJV).

A fallen church:
Come, I will show you the punishment of the great prostitute, who sits by many waters. With her the kings of the earth committed adultery, and the inhabitants of the earth were intoxicated with the wine of her adulteries.... This name written on her forehead was a mystery: BABYLON THE GREAT; THE MOTHER OF PROSTITUTES AND OF THE ABOMINATIONS OF THE EARTH. (Rev. 17:1, 2, 5)

What could cause churches who claim to be God's people to become fallen churches? It is the acceptance of doctrines that are a mixture of truth and error, which constitutes the deadly wine of Babylon. So the 144,000 is a description of the true people of God who live through the end of time and have no lie in their mouths because they have not become tainted with the false doctrines of the churches around them.

What will God's people be doing during the dangerous times of the fifth trumpet? While the winds are still being held, those who have the seal of God will be giving the last warning message to the world.

> At the commencement of the time of trouble, we were filled with the Holy Ghost as we went forth and proclaimed the Sabbath more fully. (*Early Writings*, p. 33)

> When the storm of persecution really breaks upon us, the true sheep will hear the true Shepherd's voice. Self-denying efforts will be put forth to save the lost, and many who have strayed from the fold will come back to follow the great Shepherd. The people of God will draw together and present to the enemy a united front.... Then will the message of the third angel swell to a loud cry, and the whole earth will be lightened with the glory of the Lord. (*Testimonies for the Church*, vol. 6, p. 401)

While God's people are hurrying to finish the work of the final reaping under the power of the latter rain, things upon the earth will be deteriorating. Notice some excerpts from the Biblical account of the fifth trumpet concerning those who will not be protected from the dreadful things that will be happening:

> During those days people will seek death but will not find it; they will long to die, but death will elude them. The locusts looked like horses prepared for battle.... They had breastplates like ... iron, and the sound of their wings was like the thundering of many horses and chariots rushing into battle. They had tails with stingers, like scorpions, and in their tails they had power to torment people for five months. They had as king over them the angel of the Abyss, whose name in Hebrew is Abaddon, and in Greek, Apollyon (that is, Destroyer). The first woe is past; two other woes are yet to come. (Rev. 9:6–12)

As the fifth trumpet wanes and the sixth begins to sound, the curtain of prophecy opens on the final scenes of earth's history.

> *The sixth angel sounded his trumpet,* and I heard a voice coming from the four horns of the golden altar that is before God. It said to the sixth angel who had the trumpet, 'Release the four angels who are bound at the great river Euphrates.' And the four angels

who had been kept ready for this very hour and day and month and year were released to kill a third of mankind. The number of the mounted troops was twice ten thousand times ten thousand. I heard their number. (Rev. 9:13–16, emphasis added)

It is obvious that at this time, the winds of strife will have been let go, and the result is that there is nothing to restrain the angry nations from wreaking havoc upon the earth. The days in which we live are solemn and important. The Spirit of God is gradually but surely being withdrawn from the earth. Plagues and judgments are already falling upon the despisers of the grace of God. The calamities by land and sea, the unsettled state of society, and the alarms of war are portentous. They forecast approaching events of the greatest magnitude.

> The agencies of evil are combining their forces, and consolidating. They are strengthening for the last great crisis. Great changes are soon to take place in our world, and the final movements will be rapid ones. (*Evangelism*, p. 32)

> Angels are now restraining the winds of strife, that they may not blow until the world shall be warned of its coming doom; but a storm is gathering, ready to burst upon the earth; and when God shall bid His angels loose the winds, there will be such a scene of strife as no pen can picture. (*Education*, pp. 179, 180)

> The wickedness of the inhabitants of the world has almost filled up the measure of their iniquity. This earth has almost reached the place where God will permit the destroyer to work his will upon it. The substitution of the laws of men for the law of God, the exaltation, by merely human authority, of Sunday in place of the Bible Sabbath, *is the last act in the drama*. When this substitution becomes universal, God will reveal Himself. He will arise in His majesty to shake terribly the earth. *He will come out of His place to punish the inhabitants of the world for their iniquity, and the earth shall disclose her blood and shall no more cover her slain.* (*Testimonies for the Church*, vol. 7, p. 141, emphasis added)

The closing of human probation is closely tied to the Sunday-Sabbath issue. The Sabbath is a sign of the creatorship of God, and it makes known His right to rule the universe as well as every aspect of our personal lives.

Without this understanding as an anchor, we can drift into error on other Biblical truths that might not appeal to us as well.

> There are now true Christians in every church, not excepting the Roman Catholic communion, who honestly believe that Sunday is the Sabbath of divine appointment. God accepts their sincerity of purpose and their integrity before Him. But when Sunday observance shall be enforced by law, and the world shall be enlightened concerning the obligation of the true Sabbath, then whoever shall transgress the command of God, to obey a precept which has no higher authority than that of Rome, will thereby honor popery above God. (*The Great Controversy*, p. 449)

When this happens, with the United States of America leading the way, the probation of all nations will come to an end.

> With unerring accuracy the Infinite One still keeps account with the nations. While His mercy is tendered, with calls to repentance, the account remains open; but when the figures reach a certain amount which God has fixed, the ministry of His wrath begins. The account is closed. Divine patience ceases. Mercy no longer pleads in their behalf. (*Prophets and Kings*, p. 364)

> As America, the land of religious liberty, shall unite with the papacy in forcing the conscience and compelling men to honor the false sabbath, the people of every country on the globe will be led to follow her example. (*Testimonies for the Church*, vol. 6, p. 18)

> When our nation, in its legislative councils, shall enact laws to bind the consciences of men in regard to their religious privileges, enforcing Sunday observance, and bringing oppressive power to bear against those who keep the seventh-day Sabbath, the law of God will, to all intents and purposes, be made void in our land; and national apostasy will be followed by national ruin. ("David's Prayer," *The Review and Herald*, December 18, 1888)

> When Protestantism shall stretch her hand across the gulf to grasp the hand of the Roman power, when she shall reach over the abyss to clasp hands with spiritualism, when, under the influence of this threefold union, our country shall repudiate every principle of its Constitution as a Protestant and republican

government, and shall make provision for the propagation of papal falsehoods and delusions, then we may know that the time has come for the marvelous working of Satan, and that the end is near.... As the approach of the Roman armies was a sign to the disciples of the impending destruction of Jerusalem, so may this apostasy be a sign to us that the limit of God's forbearance is reached, that the measure of our nation's iniquity is full, and that the angel of mercy is about to take her flight, never to return. (*Testimonies for the Church*, vol. 5, p. 451; see Matt. 24:24; 2 Thess. 2:9–12; Rev. 13:13; 16:14)

During the sixth trumpet (Rev. 9:13–21), torture, war, and death are everywhere, yet the unsealed people who are left do not repent of their sins, for their hearts are forever hardened against God. This is the time when the seven last plagues are being poured out upon the earth (verse 20), and the final battle of God against Satan and his followers is enacted.

The sixth angel poured out his bowl on the great river Euphrates, and its water was dried up to prepare the way for the kings from the East. Then I saw three impure spirits that looked like frogs; they came out of the mouth of the dragon, out of the mouth of the beast and out of the mouth of the false prophet. They are demonic spirits that perform signs, and they go out to the kings of the whole world, to gather them for the battle on the great day of God Almighty.... Then they gathered the kings together to the place that in Hebrew is called Armageddon. (Rev. 16:12–14, 16)

I believe this to be a real battle, which will involve all the armies of the world, led and spurred on by the devil and his evil forces.

Four mighty angels hold back the powers of this earth till the servants of God are sealed in their foreheads. The nations of the world are eager for conflict; but they are held in check by the angels. When this restraining power is removed, there will come a time of trouble and anguish. Deadly instruments of warfare will be invented.... All who have not the spirit of truth will unite under the leadership of satanic agencies. But they are to be kept under control till the time shall come for the great battle of Armageddon. Angels are belting the world, refusing Satan his claims to supremacy.... keeping the armies of Satan at bay till the sealing of God's people shall be accomplished.... The Lord is a refuge for all who put their trust in Him. He bids them hide in Him for a little moment, until the indignation shall be overpast. He is soon to come out of His place to punish the world for its iniquity. (*The Seventh-day Adventist Bible Commentary*, vol. 7, p. 967)

In the last scenes of this earth's history, war will rage. The powers of evil will not yield up the conflict without a struggle. But Providence has a part to act in the battle of Armageddon. The Captain of the Lord's host will stand at the head of the angels of heaven to direct the battle. (*Maranatha*, p. 297)

Only a moment of time, as it were, yet remains. But while already nation is rising against nation, and kingdom against kingdom, there is not now a general engagement. As yet the four winds are held until the servants of God shall be sealed in their foreheads. Then the powers of earth will marshal their forces for the last great battle. (*Testimonies for the Church*, vol. 6, p. 14)

What could possibly spark such a great battle that would involve the whole world? I personally believe that the spark that will fuel such a war could happen in the Middle East over the possession of the Temple Mount in Jerusalem. Below are a few quotations from that perspective.

Virtually every year since Israel's annexation of Arab East Jerusalem following the Six Day War in 1967, Jewish extremists armed with bombs and Bibles have stormed the gates of the mosque compound.... And some Christian fundamentalists in the United States are playing a major role.... The driving force in the United States behind efforts to rebuild the temple has come from within the 45.5 million strong Christian evangelical community. By one estimate, there are as many as 250 American Christian evangelical groups operating in the United States whose main purpose is to support Israel.... The alliance between Jewish and Christian fundamentalists is perhaps the ultimate marriage of convenience, with the two groups united to bring on the Messiah and each side convinced the Messiah will be its own.... Arab nations have promised a holy war in retaliation for any successful Jewish attempt to destroy the mosques on the Temple Mount.... Israeli experts fear that Jewish extremists are planning an incident that could spark an international conflagration. Because the Temple Mount is a focus of Muslim passions, it is an easy political instrument with which to rally the Islamic world to the defense of the faith against the infidels. A successful attack by these zealots for Zion on Muslim holy places could push humanity to the brink of a nuclear Armageddon. ("Terror on Sacred Ground," *Mother Jones*, August/September 1987)

Are there any indications from Scripture that would support this possibility? I will mention only one. Please read Daniel 11:29–45. I want to emphasize verse 45, especially: "He will pitch his royal tents between the seas at the beautiful holy mountain. Yet he will come to his end, and no one will help him." Ellen White makes this comment concerning Dan. 11:30–36: "Much of the history that has taken place in the fulfillment of this prophecy will be repeated.... Scenes similar to those described in these words will take place" (*Manuscript Releases*, vol. 13, p. 394).

"Then they gathered the kings together to the place that in Hebrew is called Armageddon" (Rev. 16:16). Interestingly, the name "Armageddon" itself has some implications. *Strong's Concordance* states that "Armageddon— Har—a short form of Harar, meaning: A mountain, hill, mount, or range of hills. Megiddow—from gadad, meaning: Rendezvous; to crowd; to assemble, or gather selves together in troops. In other words, Armageddon means "the battle for the mountain." In all of this, we can see Satan's counterfeit for God's holy mountain, His sanctuary in heaven. God says of him:

> You said in your heart, 'I will ascend to heaven; I will raise my throne above the stars of God; I will sit enthroned on the mount of assembly, on the utmost heights of Mount Zaphon.' (Isa. 14:13)

> You were on the holy mount of God; you walked among the fiery stones. You were blameless in your ways from the day you were created till wickedness was found in you.... So I drove you in disgrace from the mount of God, and I expelled you, guardian cherub, from among the fiery stones. (Ezek. 28:14–16)

Of course, it is Satan's consuming passion to get back some of his lost glory, and this he tries to do through his earthly emissaries and those who follow him. Through them he wants to rule the world, but Jesus and His angels will win that final battle. All the while, His own followers will be safe because they have responded to the call of the trumpets and have entered God's hiding place.

> I saw that God will in a wonderful manner preserve His people through the time of trouble. (*Testimonies for the Church*, vol. 1, p. 353)

> Fearful tests and trials await the people of God. The spirit of war is stirring the nations from one end of the earth to the other. But in the midst of the time of trouble that is coming,—a time of trouble such as has not been since there was a nation,—God's chosen people will stand unmoved. Satan and his host cannot destroy them, for angels that excel in strength will protect them. (*Testimonies for the Church*, vol. 9, p. 17)

> When tempted to sin, let us remember that Jesus is pleading for us in the heavenly sanctuary. When we put away our sins and come to Him in faith, He takes our names on His lips, and presents them to His Father, saying, 'I have graven them upon the palms of my hands; I know them by name.' And the command goes forth to the angels to protect them. Then in the day of fierce trial He will say, 'Come, my people, enter thou into thy chambers, and shut thy doors behind thee: hide thyself as it were for a little moment, until the indignation be overpast.' What are the chambers in which they are to hide?—They are the protection of Christ and holy angels. (*The Seventh-day Adventist Bible Commentary*, vol. 4, p. 1143)

> The LORD will roar from Zion and thunder from Jerusalem; the earth and the heavens will tremble. But the LORD will be a refuge for his people, a stronghold for the people of Israel. (Joel 3:16; see Joel 3:9–16)

> *The seventh angel sounded his trumpet*, and there were loud voices in heaven, which said: 'The kingdom of the world has become the kingdom of our Lord and of his Messiah, and he will reign for ever and ever.' And the twenty-four elders, who were seated on their thrones before God, fell on their faces and worshiped God, saying: 'We give thanks to you, Lord God Almighty, the One who is and who was, because you have taken your great power and have begun to reign. The nations were angry, and

your wrath has come. The time has come for judging the dead, and for rewarding your servants the prophets and your people who revere your name, both great and small—and for destroying those who destroy the earth.' Then God's temple in heaven was opened, and within his temple was seen the ark of his covenant. And there came flashes of lightning, rumblings, peals of thunder, an earthquake and a severe hailstorm. (Rev. 11:15–19; emphasis added)

Then will appear the sign of the Son of Man in heaven. And then all the peoples of the earth will mourn when they see the Son of Man coming on the clouds of heaven, with power and great glory. And he will send his angels with a loud trumpet call, and they will gather his elect from the four winds, from one end of the heavens to the other. (Matt. 24:30, 31)

And so the seven trumpets bring us to the culmination of earth's history. May we all be waiting and watching for that glorious day! "He who testifies to these things says, 'Yes, I am coming soon.' Amen. Come, Lord Jesus" (Rev. 22:20).

Appendix: Miscellaneous Phenomena and Signs of the End

Many events have happened in the time of the trumpets that I have not been able to include in the main text of this book. There are many more than I can list here; however, in this section are some that I have found most interesting.

These incidents occurred in late 2010 and early 2011:

Several hundred dead birds fell from the sky in Texas. Thousands of birds fell from the sky in central Arkansas. Five hundred birds fell from the sky in Louisiana. Hundreds more birds fell from the sky in Kentucky. Two million fish washed ashore in the Chesapeake Bay area. One hundred thousand fish died in the Arkansas River, covering 20 linear miles. Ninety-nine percent of the fish are only one kind, called Drum fish. One hundred tons of fish died in the waters off of Parana, Argentina. Tens of thousands of dead birds fell to the ground in Manitoba, Canada. Forty thousand crabs washed ashore in the United Kingdom. Ten thousand antelope died in Kazakhstan. These represent one-fourth of the total global population of this animal. The bees are dying out in unprecedented numbers. Eight thousand doves fell over the skies of Italy, and all had strange blue markings on their beaks. In Sweden, 100 Jackdaw crows fell to the ground.

In just one month's time, there were earthquakes in New Guinea, El Salvador, Sumatra, Japan, Fiji, Vanatu, Chili, and on the California-Mexico border, ranging from 5.6 – 7.4 in severity. "The number of tornadoes nationwide for the month [of April, 2011] was 875, the most on record, including 305 tornadoes from April 25—28 that killed at least 309 people" (*Minneapolis Star Tribune*, 2011).

An article from the December, 2003 *Idaho Observer* talks about how scientists must keep an eye on Yellowstone:

> Recent eruptions, 200 degree ground temperatures, bulging magma and 84 degree water temperatures prompt heightened scrutiny of park's geothermal activity.... Yellowstone National Park happens to be on top of one of the largest 'super volcanoes' in the world.... This next eruption could be 2,500 times the size of the 1980 Mount St. Helens eruption. Volcanologists have been tracking the movement of magma under the park and have calculated that, in parts of Yellowstone, the ground has risen over seventy centimeters this century. In July, 2003, Yellowstone Park rangers closed the entire Norris Geyser Basin because of deformation of the land and excessively high ground temperatures. There is an area that is 28 miles long by seven miles wide that has bulged upward over five inches since 1996, and this year the ground temperature on that bulge has reached over 200 degrees.... There was no choice but to close off the entire area. Everything in this area is dying: The trees, flowers, grass and shrubs. A dead zone is developing and spreading outward. The animals are literally migrating out of the park. Then during the last part of July one of the Park geologists discovered a huge bulge at the bottom of Yellowstone Lake. The bulge has already risen over 100 feet from the bottom of the lake and the water temperature at the surface of the bulge has reached 88 degrees and is still rising.... The Lake is now closed to the public. It is filled with dead fish floating everywhere. The same is true of the Yellowstone river and most of the other streams in the Park. Dead and dying fish are filling the water everywhere. Many of the picnic areas in the Park have been closed and people visiting the Park usually stay but a few hours before leaving since the stench of sulfur is so strong they literally can't stand the smell.... A source that has demonstrated first-hand knowledge of the park's history and recent geothermal events stated the following: 'The American people are not being told that the explosion of this 'super volcano' could happen at any moment. When Yellowstone does blow, some geologists predict that every living thing within six hundred miles is likely to die. The movement of magma has been detected just three-tenths of a mile below the bulging surface of the ground in Yellowstone raising concerns that this super volcano may erupt soon.'

Interesting Facts

The earthquake of Amos 1:1 occurred after Uzziah entered the temple presumptuously to burn incense, according to Josephus (see also Zech. 14:5, and 2 Chron. 26:16–20).

The fall of Jerusalem occurred after siege began by Titus during Passover in AD 70 and ended in September, during the Feast of Tabernacles. More than one million people died. There was a series of major earthquakes between AD 31 (Christ's death on the cross) and AD 70. Historian Tacitus also speaks of particularly severe hurricanes and storms in the year AD 65 (see *The Seventh-day Adventist Bible Commentary*, vol. 5, p. 497).

Mt. Vesuvius erupted on August 24, AD 79, on the festival of Vulcan, the Roman god of fire, and among the 20,000 who perished was the Roman legion that had led in the destruction of Jerusalem, who were vacationing in Pompeii.

The Lisbon earthquake occurred on November 1, 1755, All Saints' Day. An estimated 60,000 died from the quake, tidal wave, fires and aftershocks. All Saints' Day is a time when Catholics and Orthodox religions remember saints and martyrs who have died. Church attendance that day is required, and many of the people who died were at mass right as the earthquake struck.

The pope visited the United States on April 15, 2008. Many earthquakes occurred around the world from April 30–May 14, as well as other disasters—fire, floods, and tornados. The fall of United States' economy began on September 15, 2008.

In 2004, a tsunami occurred in Southeast Asia on Christmas, and 180,000 people died. December 25 is traditionally a pagan holiday for celebrating the winter solstice, when the sun begins its return to be closer to the earth. A second tsunami occurred in the same region on Easter, 2005. Easter comes from *Eostre*, the goddess of dawn, whose festival was celebrated at the spring equinox.

I believe there is a reason why God allows disasters to fall on pagan holidays, or Christianized holidays that have pagan origins. It is a reminder that at the end of the world when Jesus comes again, "the idols will totally disappear" (Isa. 2:18). God also wants to destroy our dependence upon Satan's counterfeit religious festivals and emphasize that only His day of worship and His appointed celebrations have true spiritual meaning and significance.

Blood Moons

In the Old Testament, the prophet Joel states, "The sun will be turned to darkness and the moon to blood before the coming of the great and the dreadful day of the Lord" (Joel 2:31). In the New Testament, Peter quotes this same prophecy in Acts 2:20. Jesus also speaks of it in Matthew 24:29, 30. Today numerous people are noticing that the phenomenon of blood moons is increasing.

Mark Biltz, pastor of El Shaddai Ministries in Bonney Lake, Washington, has noticed a trend in this phenomenon in this century. Here is an excerpt from an article that talks about his findings:

> During this century, tetrads [four consecutive total lunar eclipses] occur at least six times, but what's interesting is that the only string of four consecutive blood moons that coincide with God's holy days of Passover in the spring and the autumn's Feast of Tabernacles (also called Succoth) occurs between 2014 and 2015.... 'You didn't have any astronomical tetrads in the 1800s, the 1700s, the 1600s. In the 1500s, there were six, but none of those fell on Passover and Succoth.' When checking the schedule for solar eclipses, Biltz found two—one on the first day of the Hebrew year and the next on the high holy day of Rosh Hashanah, the first day of the seventh Hebrew month. Both of these take place in the 2014-2015 year. Biltz says, 'You have the religious year beginning with the total solar eclipse, two weeks later a total lunar eclipse on Passover, and then the civil year beginning with the solar eclipse followed two weeks later by another total blood red moon on the Feast of Succoth all in 2015.'

Strange Phenomena

For months strange sounds were reported in different places around the world, sounding like male voices in a choir, humming together just above the trees. I heard them myself online, and it was very eerie. The first seemed to be in the Ukraine. It reminded me of some insights from Ellen White:

> For nearly forty years after the doom of Jerusalem had been pronounced by Christ Himself, the Lord delayed His judgments upon the city and the nation.... Signs and wonders appeared, foreboding disaster and doom. In the midst of the night an unnatural light shone over the temple and the altar. Upon the clouds at sunset were pictured chariots and men of war gathering for battle. The priests ministering by night in the sanctuary were terrified by mysterious sounds; the earth trembled, and a

multitude of voices were heard crying, 'Let us depart hence.' The great eastern gate, which was so heavy that it could hardly be shut by a score of men ... opened at midnight, without visible agency. (*The Great Controversy*, p. 27, 29, 30)

Sabbatical Years

Recently some people have been noticing that the things I believe to be trumpet warnings from God to our generation are occurring on Jewish Sabbatical years. For example, the stock market crash in 1987 was in a Sabbatical year, and the years 2001, 2008, and 2015 are also Sabbatical years. As a result of this rising interest, I did some research on my own. Here is a synopsis of what I found:

> As soon as the Jews settled in the Holy Land, they began to count and observe seven-year cycles. Every cycle would culminate in a Sabbatical year, known as Shemittah, literally: 'to release.' The year following the destruction of the second Holy Temple was the first year of a seven-year Sabbatical cycle. In the Jewish calendar, counting from Creation, this was the year 3829, 68–69 CE on the secular calendar. By counting sevens from then, we see that the next Shemittah year will be the year 5775 after Creation, which runs from Sept. 25, 2014, through Sept. 13, 2015. (Chabad-Lubavitch Media Center, www.chabad.org, [accessed September 28, 2015])

The Old Testament support for the seven-year Sabbath cycle is found in these two texts:

> When you enter the land I am going to give you, the land itself must observe a sabbath to the LORD. For six years sow your fields, and for six years prune your vineyards and gather their crops. But in the seventh year the land is to have a year of sabbath rest, a sabbath to the LORD. Do not sow your fields or prune your vineyards. Do not reap what grows of itself or harvest the grapes of your untended vines. The land is to have a year of rest. (Lev. 25:2–5)

> At the end of every seven years you must cancel debts. This is how it is to be done: Every creditor shall cancel any loan they have made to a fellow Israelite. They shall not require payment

from among their own people, because the LORD's time for canceling debts has been proclaimed. (Deut. 15:1, 2)

Please notice that two important things happened in a Sabbath year: First, the land was to rest, without cultivation or harvesting; and second, "the seventh year was ... called a 'year of release' (Deut 31:10), in which the debts of poor Hebrews were to be remitted. (*The Seventh-day Adventist Bible Commentary*, vol. 8, p. 938)

I have asked myself, "Do the sabbatical years have any application or significance for us today, and why do significant events often seem to fall on those years?" We may not know all the answers to these questions, but I do believe that there is more for us to learn, as Ellen G. White states in the following quotations:

The Jewish economy is not yet fully comprehended by men today. Truths vast and profound are contained in Old Testament history. The gospel is its interpreter, the key which unlocks its mysteries. The plan of redemption is unfolding these truths to the understanding.... Let the shaft which has begun to work the mine of truth sink deep, and it will yield rich and precious treasures. (*The Ellen G. White 1888 Materials*, p. 1689)

We have yet to learn that the whole Jewish economy is a compacted prophecy of the gospel. It is the gospel in figures; for from the pillar of cloud Christ Himself presented the duty of man to his fellow man. (*Manuscript Releases*, vol. 5, p. 210)

Although the Jewish rites and symbols connected with the earthly sanctuary service were cancelled when Jesus became the High Priest in the heavenly sanctuary (see Heb. 10:19–25), there is still much to learn about the deeper meanings of the instructions and laws given for the lives of the Jewish people. The principles underlying these laws, which were given for the good of human life and the care of the earth, are still valid principles that can teach us much.

My conclusion is that the God who ordered these laws for His ancient people is the same God who is soon to come back to earth to rescue us from this dying planet. While Jesus is still ministering in the heavenly sanctuary, He is sending messages to His people to keep them in step with the progress

He is making in preparation for His coming. The Bible is written in sanctuary language, and God's people should understand it.

As we have studied in earlier chapters, the numbers "seven," and "three and one-half" have significant meaning throughout the Bible—almost like a secret code language between God and His people. When God speaks to us in sanctuary language, it is as though He is putting His personal signature upon whatever is from Him. This is imperative because the enemy also does things in the earth, and God does not want His children to be confused about who is speaking the trumpet messages and what they mean for earth's inhabitants. I believe He is using the heavenly language of timing to put His signature upon what He is allowing to happen. Unfortunately, not everyone will understand. It all depends upon the condition of the heart, and the closeness of our walk with God.

> The wise heart will know the proper time and procedure. (Eccles. 8:5)

> But when grace is shown to the wicked, they do not learn righteousness. (Isa. 26:10)

> The words are rolled up and sealed until the time of the end. Many will be purified, made spotless and refined, but the wicked will continue to be wicked. None of the wicked will understand, but those who are wise will understand. (Dan. 12:9, 10)

In my heart I sense that the seven-year Sabbath message from Jesus for us right now is:

> *My children, I want you to forgive all the grudges and hurts and wrongs that you may feel that others have committed against you. I have taken these all on the cross of Calvary for everyone. Let them go forever, for I am coming soon to get you and take you to My home to live with Me. But if you do not listen to my trumpet warnings and forgive and make things right with your fellowmen, their blood will be on your hands, and I cannot recognize you as one of my own, for you do not have my character of love. Quickly, My children! Make haste! The time is dwindling rapidly in which you can let go of everything that besets you. Money is nothing, for I will sustain you. Houses and lands are nothing, for I will provide for you. Look to Me, and I will guide you through the difficult days ahead. Please heed My voice, for there is so little time left, and I love*

you so much more than you can ever know! Above all, remember: I am coming soon!

There is one more aspect of the Jewish economy that remains to be fulfilled. It is called the year of Jubilee. "The 50th year, at the end of 7 sabbatical-year cycles (Lev. 25:8, 10), in which sowing and harvesting were forbidden (v. 11), all Hebrew slaves were to be freed (v. 10), and lands reverted to their original owners (vs. 24-28)" (*The Seventh-day Adventist Bible Commentary*, vol. 8, p. 606). This will be fulfilled at the second coming of Jesus.

> It was at midnight that God chose to deliver His people.... The sky opened and shut and was in commotion.... God spoke the day and the hour of Jesus' coming and delivered the everlasting covenant to His people.... The Israel of God stood with their eyes fixed upward, listening to the words as they came from the mouth of Jehovah.... It was awfully solemn.... And when the never-ending blessing was pronounced on those who had honored God in keeping His Sabbath holy, there was a mighty shout of victory over the beast and over his image. Then commenced the jubilee, when the land should rest. (*Early Writings*, pp. 285, 286)

Oh glorious day! The great controversy between Christ and Satan will be finished! After six thousand years of unspeakable suffering for both earth and heaven, the whole universe will rest. The seventh thousand year will be spent in a heavenly sabbatical rest for the redeemed (see Rev. 20:1–6).

> Then I saw 'a new heaven and a new earth,' for the first heaven and the first earth had passed away.... I saw the Holy City, the new Jerusalem, coming down out of heaven from God, prepared as a bride beautifully dressed for her husband. And I heard a loud voice from the throne saying, 'Look! God's dwelling place is now among the people, and he will dwell with them. They will be his people, and God himself will be with them and be their God. 'He will wipe every tear from their eyes. There will be no more death' or mourning or crying or pain, for the old order of things has passed away. (Rev. 21:1–4)

> For the Lord himself shall descend from heaven with a shout, with the voice of the archangel, and with the trump of God: and the dead in Christ shall rise first: Then we which are alive and remain shall be caught up together with them in the clouds, to

meet the Lord in the air: and so shall we ever be with the Lord. (1 Thess. 4:16, 17, KJV)

Even so, come, Lord Jesus. (Rev. 22:20, KJV)

Bibliography

Maxwell, Mervyn C. *God Cares, vol. 1.* Pacific Press Publishing Association, 1998.
White, Ellen G. *Counsels to Writers and Editors*. Nashville, TN: Southern Publishing Association, 1946.
White, Ellen G. *Christ's Object Lessons*. Review and Herald Publishing Association, 1900.
White, Ellen G. *Early Writings*. Washington D.C.: Review and Herald Publishing Association, 1882.
White, Ellen G. *Education.* Mountain View, CA: Pacific Press Publishing Association, 1903.
White, Ellen G. *Evangelism*. Washington D.C.: Review and Herald Publishing Association, 1946.
White, Ellen G. *Fundamentals of Christian Education.* Nashville, TN: Southern Publishing Association, 1923.
White, Ellen G. *Gospel Workers*. Washington D.C.: Review and Herald Publishing Association, 1915.
White, Ellen G. *In Heavenly Places*. Washington D.C.: Review and Herald Publishing Association, 1967.
White, Ellen G. *Manuscript Releases, vol. 5.* Silver Spring, MD: Ellen G. White Estate, 1990.
White, Ellen G. *Manuscript Releases, vol. 15.* Silver Spring, MD: Ellen G. White Estate, 1990.
White, Ellen G. *Maranatha*. Washington, D.C.: Review and Herald Publishing Association, 1976.
White, Ellen G. *My Life Today*. Washington D.C.: Review and Herald Publishing Association, 1952.
White, Ellen G. *Patriarchs and Prophets*. Washington D.C.: Review and Herald Publishing Association, 1890.
White, Ellen G. *Prophets and Kings.* Mountain View, CA: Pacific Press Publishing Association, 1917.

White, Ellen G. *Reflecting Christ*. Hagerstown, MD: Review and Herald Publishing Association, 1985.

White, Ellen G. *SDA Bible Commentary, vol. 4*. Washington, D.C.: Review and Herald Publishing Association, 1955.

White, Ellen G. *SDA Bible Commentary, vol. 5*. Washington, D.C.: Review and Herald Publishing Association, 1956.

White, Ellen G. *SDA Bible Commentary, vol. 7*. Washington, D.C.: Review and Herald Publishing Association, 1957.

White, Ellen G. *Selected Messages Book 2*. Washington, D.C.: Review and Herald Publishing Association, 1958.

White, Ellen G. *Selected Messages Book 3*. Washington, D.C.: Review and Herald Publishing Association, 1980.

White, Ellen G. *Spiritual Gifts, vol. 4b*. Battle Creek, MI: Seventh-day Adventist Publishing Association, 1864.

White, Ellen G. *Testimonies for the Church, vol. 1*. Mountain View, CA: Pacific Press Publishing Association, 1868.

White, Ellen G. *Testimonies for the Church, vol. 2*. Mountain View, CA: Pacific Press Publishing Association, 1871.

White, Ellen G. *Testimonies for the Church, vol. 5*. Mountain View, CA: Pacific Press Publishing Association, 1889.

White, Ellen G. *Testimonies for the Church, vol. 6*. Mountain View, CA: Pacific Press Publishing Association, 1901.

White, Ellen G. *Testimonies for the Church, vol. 7*. Mountain View, CA: Pacific Press Publishing Association, 1902.

White, Ellen G. *Testimonies for the Church, vol. 8*. Mountain View, CA: Pacific Press Publishing Association, 1904.

White, Ellen G. *Testimonies for the Church, vol. 9*. Mountain View, CA: Pacific Press Publishing Association, 1909.

White, Ellen G. *Testimonies on Sexual Behavior, Adultery, and Divorce*. Silver Spring, MD: Ellen G. White Estate, 1989.

White, Ellen G. *Testimonies to Ministers and Gospel Workers*. Mountain View, CA: Pacific Press Publishing Association, 1923.

White, Ellen G. *The Desire of Ages*. Mountain View, CA: Pacific Press Publishing Association, 1898.

White, Ellen G. *The Ellen G. White 1888 Materials*. Washington, D.C.: Ellen G. White Estate, 1987.

White, Ellen G. *The Great Controversy*. Mountain View, CA: Pacific Press Publishing Association, 1911.

White, Ellen G. *The Upward Look*. Washington D.C.: Review and Herald Publishing Association, 1982.

White, Ellen G. *This Day With God*. Washington D.C.: Review and Herald Publishing Association, 1979.

White, Ellen G. *Thoughts from the Mount of Blessing*. Mountain View, CA: Pacific Press Publishing Association, 1896.

We invite you to view the complete
selection of titles we publish at:

www.TEACHServices.com

Scan with your mobile
device to go directly
to our website.

Please write or email us your praises, reactions, or
thoughts about this or any other book we publish at:

P.O. Box 954
Ringgold, GA 30736

info@TEACHServices.com

TEACH Services, Inc., titles may be purchased in bulk for
educational, business, fund-raising, or sales promotional use.
For information, please e-mail:

BulkSales@TEACHServices.com

Finally, if you are interested in seeing
your own book in print, please contact us at

publishing@TEACHServices.com

We would be happy to review your manuscript for free.

www.ingramcontent.com/pod-product-compliance
Lightning Source LLC
Chambersburg PA
CBHW070543170426
43200CB00011B/2533